The Making of the Morgan

The Making of the Morgan

FROM

Charles McKim

TO

Renzo Piano

Paul Spencer Byard

Cynthia Davidson

Charles E. Pierce, Jr.

Brian Regan

THE MORGAN LIBRARY & MUSEUM, NEW YORK

This publication was generously underwritten by the
Franklin Jasper Walls Lecture Fund.

LIBRARY OF CONGRESS CATALOGING-IN-PUBLICATION DATA
The making of the Morgan from Charles McKim to Renzo Piano /
Paul S. Byard ... [et al.].
    p. cm.
 Includes bibliographical references.
 ISBN 978-0-87598-149-9 (alk. paper)
  1. Pierpont Morgan Library—History. 2. McKim, Charles Follen,
1847–1909. 3. Piano, Renzo. 4. Library architecture—New York
(State)—New York. 5. Morgan, J. Pierpont (John Pierpont),
1837–1913—Art patronage. 6. New York (N.Y.)—Buildings, structures,
etc. I. Byard, Paul Spencer. II. Pierpont Morgan Library.
 Z733.N733M35 2008
 727'.8217471—dc22

                                     2008038808

ISBN: 978-0-87598-149-9

FRONT COVER: Entrance to The Morgan Library & Museum

BACK COVER: Original entrance to Pierpont Morgan's library

FRONTISPIECE: The Madison Avenue entrance

PAGES 6–7: Bird's-eye view of the Morgan campus following the expansion, as seen from the west
side of Madison Avenue and 36th Street

PAGE 12: Interior of the Gilbert Court, facing south

PAGE 20: Rotunda, facing the East Room

PAGE 32: Interior of the Gilbert Court, facing south

PAGE 80: Renzo Piano, S. Parker Gilbert, and Charles E. Pierce, Jr.

PAGE 108: Niche with sculpture at the library's entrance

Printed in the United States of America

Distributed by W. W. Norton & Company, Inc.
500 Fifth Avenue, New York NY 10110
www.wwnorton.com

W. W. Norton & Company Ltd.
Castle House, 75/76 Wells Street, London W1T 3QT

Contents

Forewords

Renzo Piano's expansion and renovation of The Morgan Library & Museum have dramatically extended an architectural legacy that began a century ago. *The Making of the Morgan from Charles McKim to Renzo Piano* provides a record of that legacy and a rich account of Piano's scheme, while emphasizing the Morgan's enduring commitment to excellence, quality, and the highest standards.

With the commissioning of a personal library for his collections, Pierpont Morgan simultaneously added to them through the art of architecture. Designed by the American-Renaissance master Charles Follen McKim, the Italianate building was an immediate New York landmark. As the institution has evolved and expanded over the years, that splendid structure has remained at its core.

Renzo Piano's scheme for the Morgan brought the diverse old buildings, including the iconic original library, into practical and pleasing cohesion. More than anything else, the Piano-designed expansion has dramatically improved the Morgan's capacity to serve as a premier center for the preservation, study, and exhibition of medieval and Renaissance illuminated manuscripts, printed books, literary, historical, and music manuscripts, old master and modern drawings, and other important works.

Among these stellar collections is the manuscript of one of the most beautifully observed of all writings about architecture, Ruskin's *Stones of Venice*. In his introduction, Ruskin said:

> *Now a building, like a human being, has two distinct kinds of goodness or excellency:*
> *1. The first that it do its duty well;*
> *2. The second that it is graceful & pleasing in the doing of it.*

Ruskin's words resonate, I think, in what Renzo Piano has achieved for the Morgan. The building does its duty well—serving the public and scholars of the international community far better in the twenty-first century than ever before—and it does so in a notably graceful and pleasing manner.

WILLIAM M. GRISWOLD
Director

The Morgan developed notably during the closing decades of the twentieth century. First and foremost, the collections grew through the generosity of Trustees, Fellows, and others. As a result, the vaults were close to overflowing. With the introduction of CORSAIR, the Morgan's electronic catalog, the collections became readily available to scholars throughout the world, exponentially increasing demand thereto in various formats. Exhibitions offered at the Morgan and elsewhere also increased in number and scope, with visitorship doubling during the 1990s. These circumstances determined the essential goals of the expansion, which were greater and improved collection storage, an enhanced reading room to serve scholars, an auditorium or hall for concerts and lectures, additional gallery space to display the permanent holdings and those borrowed from elsewhere, and a new entrance, as well as other initiatives that you will read about in *The Making of the Morgan*.

The Morgan turned to Renzo Piano to help realize these programmatic aims. One of the greatest challenges posed to Renzo was both to preserve and to integrate the landmark buildings. When we began to work together, I asked him to respect the essence and the scale of the landmarks as well as the time-honored ethos of the institution—intimacy, elegance, and serenity. Our principal goal—to offer close contact with great works of human accomplishment in a setting treasured for its intimate scale— guided our planning and decisions relating to the Morgan's new architecture.

The year 2006 marked both the completion of the Piano addition and the hundredth anniversary of the opening of the original library for Pierpont Morgan's personal use. The Morgan thus celebrated a major milestone as it inaugurated a new era. In both instances, I believe we honored our generous, forward-looking founders, for in Piano's bold plan, classical and modern architecture were brought together persuasively to bring this cultural institution into the twenty-first century.

CHARLES E. PIERCE, JR.

Charles E. Pierce, Jr., was director of the Morgan from 1987 until his retirement at the end of 2007.

How best to tell the story of the Morgan expansion designed by Renzo Piano? That was the challenge we set for ourselves in planning this publication. We quickly concluded that a book about the Piano expansion must also provide ample historical context. The need for a wide-ranging historical perspective asserted itself early because, among other reasons that should become apparent in these chapters, Pierpont Morgan's original library, the Annex, and the former nineteenth-century brownstone home of J. P. Morgan, Jr., became the set pieces and point of departure for Piano's new architecture. This chronological—as well as architectural—framework also gave rise to the book's title.

The Making of the Morgan has five parts. Charles Pierce's essay considers Pierpont Morgan's motivation in forming the collections and building a library to house them. He also reflects on J. P. Morgan, Jr.'s intentions in transforming the once private domain into a public institution, its evolution, and its later development.

I offer both a chronological survey of the historic buildings and an extended essay that traces the 2006 expansion from inception to completion. The latter describes, from the client's perspective, an almost eight-year undertaking. It traces our sometimes crooked path—as in virtually all major architectural ventures, there was no direct route between aspiring to commission a building and realizing it.

In an interview with Renzo Piano by architectural writer Cynthia Davison, we hear the architect's own voice. He reflects upon accepting the Morgan commission, his perceptions of the Morgan that he encountered in 2000, the sources of his inspiration, and his vision for the project—his first in New York to be completed.

The book concludes with a historical interpretation of the Morgan's architecture, including the Piano expansion project, by the late Paul Spencer Byard, architect, architectural historian, and an authority on building additions.

I am grateful to those who helped to bring The Making of the Morgan to completion: Karen Banks, Giorgio Bianchi, Kendall Doerr, Patricia Emerson, Glory Jones, Christine Nelson, Marilyn Palmeri, Robert Parks, Frank Prial, Mary Rembold, Richard Southwick, Kristina Stillman, Michael Wetstone, and William Voelkle.

BRIAN REGAN
Deputy Director

Milestones

By 1853
Three brownstone houses erected on the eastern side of Madison Avenue between 36th and 37th Streets (Fig. 1).

1881
Pierpont Morgan purchases the brownstone owned by the Phelps family on the corner of 36th Street and Madison for his residence (Fig. 2).

1888
Addition of fourth floor and renovation to the house at Madison and 37th Street. *Architect:* R. H. Robertson

1903
Pierpont Morgan purchases the middle brownstone from the Dodge family. It was subsequently razed, and a garden designed by Beatrix Farrand was created on the lot (Fig. 3).

1904
Pierpont Morgan purchases the house owned by the Stokes family on the corner of 37th Street and Madison Avenue for his son, J. P. Morgan, Jr.

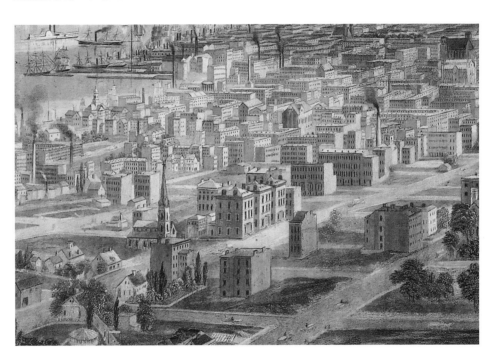

Fig. 1. Three Madison Avenue brownstones as they appeared in the middle of the nineteenth century

(*Above*) Fig 2. Home of Pierpont Morgan at the corner of Madison Avenue and 36th Street, ca. 1907

(*Right*) Fig. 3. From north to south, the three brownstones before 1903; Pierpont Morgan's was the southernmost

Fig. 4. Pierpont Morgan's library shortly after it
was completed in 1906

Fig. 5. The Annex, 1930s

Fig. 6. The Meeting Room, part of the additions
made in 1962

1906

Pierpont Morgan opens his private library
next to his residence on 36th Street (Fig. 4).
Architect: McKim, Mead & White; Charles
McKim, partner in charge

1924

J. P. Morgan, Jr., establishes The Pierpont
Morgan Library with an indenture of trust.

1928

The Pierpont Morgan Library opens the
Annex (with connecting link, called the
Cloister, to the Library) on the site of
Pierpont Morgan's former house, on
36th Street and Madison Avenue (Fig. 5).
Architect: Benjamin Wistar Morris

1944

United Lutheran Church in America purchases the J. P. Morgan, Jr., house from his
estate.

Fig. 7. The Morgan campus after the acquisition of the
Morgan House and creation of the linking Garden Court

1962
Meeting Room added above and exhibition gallery behind the Cloister and Annex (Fig. 6).
Architect: Alexander Perry Morgan

1976
Vault and offices added to rear of Annex.
Architect: Platt Wyckoff Coles

1989
The Morgan Library purchases the former J. P. Morgan, Jr., house from the Lutheran Church.

1991
Renovated Morgan house, Garden Court, and additional spaces open (Fig. 7).
Architect: Voorsanger & Associates

1996
Drawing Study Center opens on the renovated second floor of the Annex.
Architect: Beyer Blinder Belle

1999
Thaw Conservation Center opens on the rehabilitated fourth floor of the Morgan House (Fig. 8).
Architect: Samuel Anderson

2003–06
Comprehensive expansion and renovation project undertaken. Connecting link from Annex, later vault and office addition, and Morgan House annex built by Lutheran Church removed (Fig. 9).
Architect: Renzo Piano Building Workshop

Fig. 8. The Thaw Conservation Center

(*Following pages*) Fig. 9. The Madison Avenue entrance

Private to Public: Opening Mr. Morgan's Library to All

CHARLES E. PIERCE, JR.

In 1900 Pierpont Morgan was "a master of the universe." On both sides of the Atlantic, he was widely regarded as the most brilliant and influential financier of his time. Having borrowed immense amounts of European capital to invest in America's industrial expansion, he helped fuel America's industrial revolution after the Civil War. He joined with others to forge major corporations in railroad, electricity, and steel, to name just a few, and was an influential voice in various issues of national economic policy. Many people considered Morgan the second most powerful man in America after the president (Fig. 10).

Moreover, between 1890 and 1900, Morgan had become the greatest private collector of European art in America. He had always been an instinctive collector, even as a boy, but after the death of his father in 1890, he gave free rein to his desire to possess the most beautiful and important artifacts of the great civilizations of western Europe and the ancient Near East (Fig. 11). Determined to buy only the best and willing to pay whatever it cost, he bought manuscripts and books, drawings and paintings, decorative objects and sculpture as well as ancient Assyrian seals and Egyptian papyri. Medieval and Renaissance illuminated manuscripts; literary, historical, and scientific manuscripts; Gutenberg Bibles; old master paintings and drawings from the fourteenth to the eighteenth century; and approximately four thousand decorative objects filled his London townhouse at 13 Princes Gate (Fig. 12) and his brownstone at 219 Madison Avenue in New York. Morgan deserved to be called, as he often was in the press, Lorenzo the Magnificent.

By the turn of the century, Morgan's houses in London and New York could no longer hold all of his treasures. It was thus not surprising that he began to consider building his own library. We do not know if he ever seriously considered building such a structure in London. We do know, however, that he decided to build a library on some land next to his brownstone at the corner of Madison Avenue and 36th Street in New York. In retrospect, this choice was perhaps inevitable because Morgan, in spite of his love for Europe and its culture, was at heart an American. Although he spent many months living abroad, traveling extensively through England, France, Germany, and Italy and cruising through the Mediterranean, he nevertheless thought of New York as his home and as the center of his business life.

There were, however, at least two other reasons for his decision. The first was financial. In 1897 the United States government had passed a revenue act that had levied a 20 percent tax on imported works of art. There was, however, a provision, as Jean Strouse has pointed out, whereby "books and manuscripts could come to America duty-free as long as they were used for religious, educational, scientific, philosophical, or literary purposes." In addition, "not more than two copies could be listed in any one invoice, and the items could not be offered for sale. Since Morgan was buying single copies of rare books and manuscripts that he did not intend to sell, he could bring his literary collections to the United States without paying the import tax."[1] By 1900 Morgan had brought so many of his books to New York that he had been forced to store them in the basement of his townhouse or at the Lenox Library uptown.

The second reason was cultural. Morgan wished to bring to America as many of the finest objects of European civilization as he could in order to dramatize its achievement as well as to offer the American public the opportunity to learn from it. As Strouse astutely observed, Morgan sought "to harvest 'the best' of the world's cultural past for the American future. In stocking U.S. institutions with great works of literature and art, he was providing historical records, setting scholarly standards, and marking directions for future research."[2] He wanted to do for America what so many of the great collectors of art had done in England, France, and Italy, namely to own, preserve, and celebrate what Matthew Arnold had called in *Culture and Anarchy* (1869) "the best that has been known and thought" in European culture.

After an unsatisfactory start with another architect (Fig. 13), Morgan approached Charles McKim, who was already well known and respected as the leading proponent of Italian Renaissance architecture in America. From the start, Morgan had clear intentions

· FRONT · ELEVATION ·
· SCALE ⅜ INCH=1 FOOT ·
· PROPOSED · LIBRARY · MVSEVM · FOR ·
· J · PIERPONT · MORGAN · ESQ · NEW · YORK ·

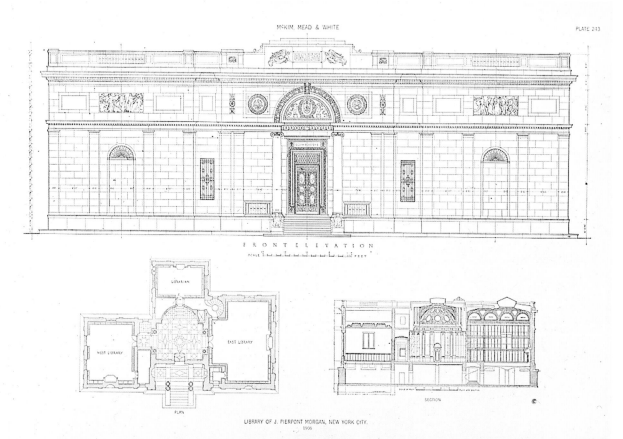

FRONT ELEVATION

PLAN   SECTION

LIBRARY OF J. PIERPONT MORGAN, NEW YORK CITY.
1906

for the library, which he conveyed to McKim. He had recently bought most of the land on the north side of 36th Street between his own house and Park Avenue. He wanted it set in a garden with ample space on both sides. In style, it should be classical and restrained on the outside, but inside it should be more elegant and ornate. Morgan wanted an office for himself and one for his librarian as well as a reading room for scholars. And he was insistent that the reading room not be designed as a "picture gallery," even though he owned a number of great paintings by many of the most celebrated European masters.

McKim gave Morgan all that he asked for (Fig. 14). Working closely together, they produced the iconic building that became known as Mr. Morgan's Library (Fig. 15). A

November 19, 1908, *London Times* article with a New York dateline celebrated the library as a "bookman's paradise" and "the most carefully guarded treasure-house in the world." And then, in a fit of hyperbole, went on to herald Morgan as "probably the greatest collector of things splendid and beautiful and rare who has ever lived."

Despite the brilliance of its architecture and importance of its collections, it was not clear what Morgan had in mind for the future of his library. He said almost nothing about these matters. As a result, we can only infer his sense of the library's purpose from how he used it during the last seven years of his life.

It is important to bear in mind that Morgan built his library next to his private residence, permitting him to treat it as an addition or extension to his home. This was a private world, his home away from home, where he could play solitaire, meet friends, conduct business, and enjoy his great books and manuscripts. It became the place to which this intensely private man went to think, solve problems, and enjoy his collections. Increasingly, during his last years, he chose not to go to 23 Wall Street but rather to hold his important business meetings in the library. It was here, for example, that the Panic of 1907 was resolved when Morgan locked the leading bankers of his day in his office until they agreed upon a plan to avert a national financial crisis.

It is equally important to remember that McKim's design for the library's ground floor gave almost equal space to Morgan's office and to his library. Together these two rooms, with their very different functions, came to represent Morgan's two most important roles: the greatest financier and greatest collector of his time.

There is no doubt that Morgan thought of his library primarily as a place for books and manuscripts, not as a gallery for paintings and decorative works. (There were, however, many important pictures and objets d'art in his office.) For this reason, he was right to call the building where he stored these works a library rather than a museum or collection. He wanted to make clear that his collections centered primarily around the written word—from ancient seals and papyri to manuscripts (illuminated and otherwise) to printed books.

There is also no doubt that Morgan thought of his library as a private preserve, primarily for his family, friends, and scholars. He enjoyed entertaining his friends there, showing them a Gutenberg Bible or his favorite illuminated manuscript, the Farnese Hours. In 1905 he appointed Belle da Costa Greene the first director of the library to screen the credentials of all those who sought to do research and to act almost literally as a guardian at the gate (Fig. 16). Morgan's library most closely resembled the Royal Library at Windsor, a royal collection to which only a fortunate few could gain access. To no one, with the possible exception of his only son, Jack, did he ever indicate that his library should become a public institution.

After Pierpont Morgan died in Rome, on March 31, 1913, Jack received the bulk of his estate and became the senior partner of JPMorgan (Fig. 17). He also inherited his father's library and collections, which were then valued at about $60 million. Jack immediately became involved in settling his father's estate. To pay various taxes, he sold a

Fig. 16. Belle da Costa Greene, 1911

Fig. 17. J. P. Morgan, Jr.

number of important paintings, many of which were subsequently bought by major collectors like Henry Clay Frick. He gave his father's extraordinary collection of decorative objects to the Wadsworth Atheneum in Hartford, in recognition of his family's long association with that city. At the same time, he decided that all of his father's books and manuscripts as well as a small number of his favorite objects, like the *Running Eros, Holding a Torch* (Fig. 18), should remain in the library. All of this took some time, and in retrospect it seems clear that each of these actions may well have been leading to his historic decision to convert the library into a public institution. He did so in a letter dated February 15, 1924, addressed to the Trustees (four of whom were family members and two of whom were close friends).

In this letter, Jack explained that he wanted, first and foremost, to create a memorial to his father and his great love of rare books and manuscripts. He wrote: "My father's interest and satisfaction in the library, which he left me, makes it a peculiarly fitting

memorial to him. It is a memorial which keeps alive the memory of his love of rare books and manuscripts and his belief in the educational value of the collection which he had gathered." He also made clear that he was now doing what he felt his father had always planned to do. "Since his death in 1913, I have constantly endeavored to see that the library and its contents should be made available in every way possible for the advancement of knowledge and for the use of learned men of all countries as he delighted to do, thus carrying out the plan which he had in mind in making the collections." Jack, in short, sought to honor his father as a collector and to fulfill his father's ultimate plan for the mission of his library.

In an attached document, entitled "Indenture of Trust," Jack articulated "the nature, object, and purposes of the institution to be founded." He defined it as "a public library, for reference only, without any circulating or withdrawal privileges . . . the object and purposes of which institution are to preserve, protect, and give permanence to the collections hereby transferred and hereafter acquired, to render them available . . . to scholars and persons engaged in the work of research and to those interested in literature, art, and kindred subjects, to disseminate and contribute to the advancement of useful information and knowledge, to encourage and develop study and research and generally to conduct an institution of educational value to the public." In this same document, he revealed that he had endowed the library with a gift of $1.5 million. (The value of the collections of the newly public library was put at $8.5 million.) It is hard to imagine how Jack could have better expressed both the letter and the spirit of what we believe was his father's aim in forming his collections and in building his library.

It was, however, just over a year later that Jack started to put his own personal mark upon the institution. On March 15, 1925, he wrote the architect Benjamin Wistar Morris as follows: "Desiring to give the library more room, both for exhibitions and for the work of students, I wish to build on the site of my father's old house, at 219 Madison Avenue, a building which shall communicate with the present library building." There are two important convictions implicit in this explanation to Morris. First, Jack wished to build an addition to his father's library because it no longer had enough space, just as Pierpont had earlier built his library because he had run out of space. Furthermore, Jack was willing to tear down his father's brownstone, rather than adapt it or build elsewhere, in order to accomplish this goal. It is hard not to think that part of Jack's motivation was to chart a more independent course from his father than he had to date. Second, and perhaps even more important, was Jack's desire to create more room both for scholars to do research and for the general public to view exhibitions. He was most explicit on this point to Morris. "The new building," he wrote in the same letter, "is to contain a large exhibition room, probably two stories in height, and also a room of smaller size, which should be used as a lecture room and seat probably thirty or forty people. There should be also sufficient room in which the students could do their work in connection with the library." In stating his goals to Morris, Jack had dramatically redefined the institution's mission going forward. It was to be both a research library *and* a museum. A reading room would serve the scholars; an exhibition gallery and a lecture room would serve the general public. And so, not long after converting his father's private preserve into a public resource, the dutiful son took the bold step of broadening its mandate.

Jack had chosen Morris for this task because he had admired the Junius Spencer Morgan Memorial that the architect had designed in 1910 for the Wadsworth Atheneum in Hartford. In particular, Jack liked the way that Morris had integrated the new Morgan Memorial with the old Atheneum building. He wanted him to achieve a similar type of integration at the Library in New York.

It is clear from their surviving notes and correspondence that the architect understood what his client wanted—and did his best to give him just that. It is also clear from these documents, especially those of April and May 1926, that the development of the design was a highly cooperative effort. The team consisted of Mr. Morgan, Miss Greene (the director), Miss Thurston (her assistant), Mr. Morris (the architect), and Mr. O'Connor (his assistant). It appears that there was little or no disagreement about Jack's goals, including the decision to raze his father's house, starting in January 1927. Jack himself was keenly involved in all aspects of the project: he was equally involved in "the perspective and general character of the exterior and the general arrangement of the interior." He reviewed carefully the drawings that showed "the relationship between the present library and the new wing" as well as those that related to the architectural details of the interior spaces. What is equally noteworthy is the degree to which Belle Greene sought to implement Jack's new mission for the library. She conceived of the general layout for the reading room, including the gallery, and expressed strong views about its look and feel. At the same time, she was equally attentive to the design of the exhibition room, including the movable exhibition cases that were modeled on some she had seen at The Metropolitan Museum of Art. The architectural details and furnishings of both rooms continued to be discussed by Morgan, Greene, and Morris until the opening on October 1, 1928.

The Annex, as it came to be called, of The Pierpont Morgan Library opened to great acclaim. It was widely and well reviewed by the press in New York and Boston. A visitor to the newly expanded library would have been struck at first by two external changes: the size of the complex had doubled, and there was a new entrance. He would have entered not through the great doors of the original library at 33 East 36th Street but through a new entrance at 29 East 36th Street. As a result, the center of gravity of the institution, as it were, had shifted from Mr. Morgan's library to his son's Annex. The private entrance had been replaced by a public one. (A long corridor or "cloister" connected the two buildings.) But this same visitor might have been even more impressed by the internal changes. After he had arrived in the front hall with its beautiful marble floors and walls, he could turn right and enter the reading room or turn left and enter the exhibition room. If he were especially observant, he would have noticed that each room was almost the same size. The equal size and weight given to the function of each room in the design of the ground floor of the Annex was Morris's solution to Jack's plan. It was also the architectural expression of the dual mission of the library.

It should now be clear that Pierpont Morgan and his son, Jack, were indeed the true founders of The Pierpont Morgan Library. It was the two of them, father and son, who, over twenty years, defined the institution's basic mission as both a research library of the humanities for scholars and as a museum for the general public. Jack respected his father's original conception of the library as a mecca for scholars but broadened it to invite the general public to enjoy whatever exhibitions and public programs it might offer. He transformed his father's library from a private treasure house into a public palace of art, into an "institution of educational value to the public." This was the mission of the library in 1928; this is still the mission of the Morgan today. It has informed the judgments of the Board of Trustees and the decisions of all four directors to date— Belle Greene, Frederick Adams, Charles Ryskamp, and myself. And it has shaped much of the thinking of all of the architects who have contributed additions and renovations to the two original buildings from 1928 to the present day. It exerted as well a profound influence upon my first discussion with Renzo Piano in July 2000—and many times thereafter—about the goals of the project that we have since undertaken and completed.

1. Jean Strouse, *Morgan: American Financier*, New York, 1999, p. 487.

2. Ibid., p. 486.

Clare Eddy
Gallery

Bringing the Morgan into the Twenty-First Century: Observations from the Inside

BRIAN REGAN

MIRACLES?

"It's a miracle, I'm telling you," claimed Renzo Piano, "nothing less than a miracle." We had walked, in early 2005, through the future Madison Avenue entrance and into the fully formed, but not entirely enclosed, central court. "Charlie, Brian, think about it: Only a few years ago these were thoughts and plans, and now they're becoming real. How can that not be a miracle?" In wonder he added, "Ever since I was a boy, I thought a building site was a miracle. I'll die thinking that."[1]

Visiting the construction site with Renzo Piano was like being with a god and a child all at once. By the time of this tour with Morgan director, Charles E. Pierce, Jr., and several of our colleagues, the three new pavilions Piano designed had taken shape. The steel and glass cladding of the office pavilion was near completion, and some of the roof structure high atop the court had been layered on its steel frame. We descended from street level and walked through the shell of the area that would comprise the vault, lobby, and education center.

Outside the embryonic auditorium, Renzo pointed up to bunched wires and unenclosed ventilation ducts. "See, these things are like the veins of the body and circulatory system. A building is alive, I'm telling you, brought to life by a miracle." Back at street level, we again surveyed the central court. Renzo remarked how pleased he was by its height. In a winning admission, he said that it felt larger than he expected—that even the architect cannot always imagine how an enclosed space will be experienced until it is constructed. Walking into what would become the Thaw Gallery, Piano irrepressibly imagined future exhibitions, suggesting how many—actually, how few, so as not to crowd the space—objects to display therein.

NOT "AERY NOTHING:" CONSTRUCTION

Rapturous as Renzo was about progress on the project, it was not, as Charlie Pierce liked to say, borrowing from Theseus in *A Midsummer Night's Dream*, formed of "aery nothing." It was miraculous only rhetorically. Renzo, of course, knew this, but his penchant for metaphor, like his enthusiasm, constitutes generous portions of his charisma.

Preliminary planning had started as early as 1998. As it developed, two dominant forces emerged that drove and shaped the expansion and renovation. Advancing the Morgan's programs and services and providing for optimal collection presentation and storage through enhanced facilities was primary. Commissioning new architecture of distinction was also an aspiration. This second consideration arose from both an appreciation of the Morgan's storied architectural history and a far broader contemporary phenomenon.

Pierpont Morgan had decided to erect a library for his personal use over one hundred years earlier. The commission that he gave to Charles McKim would make the art of architecture genitive to the institution. And McKim's sublime structure remains at the Morgan's heart.

In our own time, museums and libraries are among the most celebrated building types. As was true of the ancient temple, medieval cathedral, or Renaissance or baroque church, such projects attract gifted architects, public and professional attention, and architecture's irreducible requirement—patronage.

Those of us planning the Morgan's future were inevitably conscious of this prevailing focus upon the architecture of cultural institutions. And while there was never an intention to commission the "destination architecture" that has been raised abundantly around the globe in the past decade or so, there was a distinct hope for architecture worthy of the Morgan's legacy that was still significant in its own right. Here follows an episodic account of planning the Morgan's expansion and renovation. It is related, I hope, with candor and appreciation for the participants—many people with diverse skills and capacities—who united to make architecture.

PROLOGUE

Throughout 1998 the president of the Board of Trustees, S. Parker Gilbert, and Charlie Pierce talked frequently about the Morgan's programs and services and how effectively they were realized in the extant facilities. Late that year, they discussed these matters more formally with other Trustees. They agreed that it was the right time to move forward with evaluation and planning.

A decade of institutional growth, including several building and renovation projects, increased public offerings, and notable collection acquisitions, had validated the previous expansion of the late 1980s that had been precipitated by the purchase of the former J. P. Morgan, Jr., house.[2] In 1944, a year after the death of J. P. Morgan, Jr., the Lutheran Church acquired the Morgan house from his heirs. A decade later, the church appended a utilitarian office building to the rear of the house. Both structures were part of the parcel that church officials decided to sell in the mid-1980s and the Morgan was desperate to purchase. Collection, program, and staff growth had resulted in a facility that was, a Morgan Trustee said, "bursting at the seams," and the opportunity to expand on adjacent property felt like nothing else but an institutional imperative. Following the $15 million purchase, the Morgan retained Voorsanger Architects to join the 1928 Annex with the Morgan house. Voorsanger planned a glass and steel garden court to link the southern part of the complex with the Morgan house. The rooms of the house were renovated for use as offices, program rooms, and a new shop, and a café was opened in the court. The space gained by these measures freed up other existing rooms to serve as galleries. In 1991, the Morgan's space needs had been met for the time being. By the decade's

SUMMARY OF PROGRAM GOALS

State-of-the-art collection storage center

More gallery space for featured exhibitions and the permanent collections

A new reading room with electronic services

A dedicated auditorium / performance hall

More welcoming public entrance and improved internal circulation

An education center

Interactive learning stations

Increased storage space for reference books and materials

Modestly larger shop and dining amenities

Enclosed loading dock

Back-of-the-house storage

close, the house's fourth floor was dramatically rehabilitated to create The Thaw Conservation Center, designed by Samuel Anderson Architect. The 1991 developments, along with the program growth they fostered, set the stage for what was to come. But this earlier expansion had also left a bit of unfinished business in the form of the dour, brick annex the Lutherans built during the 1950s. The Morgan deferred, mostly for financial reasons, renovating or integrating it for program purposes. With the Morgan's healthy fiscal condition and with almost everyone sanguine about the economy and fund-raising prospects, by the late 1990s it seemed opportune to address the usefulness of the office building as well as the utility of other spaces throughout the complex.

A second planning phase provided a more trenchant analysis of museum activities and library services, capacities, and utilization rates.[3] The administrative team projected future development and sketched a broad desideratum. In a series of exchanges, staff and Trustees identified, clarified, and endorsed goals. These goals became the project's DNA. Once set, these elements, to a remarkable degree, survived many tests. The Morgan also drafted statements pertaining to qualitative aspirations for new architecture, which included commentaries on scale, ethos, and aesthetics. (They are excerpted in the sidebars.) The Morgan next retained Beyer Blinder Belle as architectural planners to examine the building envelope available for expansion. Taking institutional goals into consideration, Beyer Blinder Belle offered schematic possibilities for the site.[4]

THE LANDMARK FACTOR

Any significant changes to the complex would be subject to the review and approval of the New York City Landmarks Preservation Commission; the campus carries a number of designations. Both the exterior and interior of the McKim building have local and national protection. In 1966 the Landmarks Preservation Commission listed the original library and 1928 Annex. A year before, in the wake of the destruction of Pennsylvania Station, the Morgan House was among the nascent commission's first designations, accelerated by rumors that it might be razed by the Lutheran Church, its owner since 1944. Although the house had been designated, the church group argued in the courts that landmark status, inhibiting extensive alterations or commercial development, was a financial burden. The designation was overturned in 1974. The Lutheran Church pondered options but ultimately moved its headquarters from New York, setting the scene for the purchase of the house by Morgan Trustees in 1988.

During the years following the house's de-designation, the Landmarks Preservation Commission watched for an opportunity to reclaim it. When the Morgan project of the late 1990s was broached, Jennifer Raab, the sitting commissioner, made known an interest in the house. Along with its legal counsel, the Morgan began preliminary discussions with Commissioner Raab and her colleagues.[5]

The exchange between the Morgan and the commission became a matter of polite gamesmanship. There was small doubt about the outcome. The Morgan wanted smooth passage through the review process, leading to the commission's support for the expansion scheme. And the commission wanted to relist the Morgan House. Although, as Charlie admitted, the Morgan "didn't regard the building as an architectural marvel," it readily acknowledged its historicity as a rare survivor of its type (the freestanding, brownstone house) as well as its indissoluble association with the Morgan family and the institution's origins. The Morgan also began consensus building among preservation, architectural, and community groups that could be supportive in securing approval of new construction that would affect the house and the other historic buildings.

ARCHITECTURAL COMPETITION

Parker and Charlie, consulting with others, concluded that the significance of the architectural venture they contemplated called for some form of competition. Parker appointed a building committee that was also charged with recommending an architect to the Board of Trustees.[6] At the encouragement of Morgan Trustee Ladislaus von Hoffman, the committee retained an advisor in order to attain a fuller understanding of the current architectural scene, screen materials that would be distributed to competitors, and respond to specialized issues it was likely to encounter. Pulitzer Prize–winning critic and architectural historian Paul Goldberger was chosen. In building committee meetings, Goldberger, allowing the Morgan players to follow their own lead, filled in and rounded out their knowledge and appreciation.

The committee gathered in August 1999 to review materials that Morgan staff had assembled from the thirty or so firms mentioned by Trustees, in addition to those identified by the Morgan's senior staff in conversations with professionals in the design, museum, and library fields. Images of the firms' completed buildings, culled from books, monographs, journals, and magazines, were studied and discussed.

Having intended to select six semifinalists, the committee chose seven: Steven Holl Architects; Buttrick, White & Burtis; Beyer Blinder Belle; José Rafael Moneo; Tod Williams Billie Tsien Architects; Hugh Hardy of Hardy Holzman Pfeiffer Associates; and Arata Isozaki & Associates.

Over three days in fall 1999, these firms made presentations in the Morgan House. Some used slides, others worked from drawings. Although they were asked not to address the Morgan scheme specifically, some elected to offer preliminary thoughts about a schematic design. The latter brought no advantage, as the committee had instructed that it was interested in gaining an understanding of the architect's body of work, working method, and notions about the designer-client relationship. It became evident from the interviews that there was great enthusiasm within the profession about the Morgan project.

THREE FINALISTS

In discussions over the next month, the committee settled on three finalists: Hugh Hardy, Steven Holl, and Tod Williams and Billie Tsien. Hardy, well known in the architectural community, had in his favor a reputation for projects with a historic preservation component. Furthermore, he designed an addition to the Fenimore Art Museum in Coopers-town, which houses the collection of Native American artifacts assembled by Eugene and Clare Thaw. Many people, including Morgan Trustee Gene Thaw, were impressed by Hardy's Cooperstown scheme and the galleries for display of the Thaw collection.

Holl's architecture was the most progressive of the semifinalists. His daring schemes for a large museum in Helsinki and Seattle's Bellevue Museum piqued the committee's interest, as did his work at the Cranbrook Center for Art in Michigan. The luminous interior of Holl's Chapel of St. Ignatius at the University of Seattle had also attracted attention.

Williams and Tsien also had notable projects at Cranbrook. Their design for the new home of the Museum of Arts and Crafts on 53rd Street in New York, then in the early stages of construction, was admired by critics, as were their refined residential commissions. The firm's scheme for the Neurosciences Institute in La Jolla demon-strated a potent architectural intelligence. When the Morgan polled peers for the names of firms to consider for the project, Williams and Tsien was among the most frequently suggested.

The choice of finalists affirmed the committee's initial inclination that the new architecture for the Morgan was likely to be in a contemporary mode rather than some form of classical revival. Of the three, only Hardy, given his previous handling of expan-sions, might have been expected to provide either a historic or modern response.

The Morgan issued program requirements to the finalists and asked them to develop plans whose construction and professional fees were not to exceed $34 million. Three months following their selection, after frequent site visits and exchanges with Morgan staff, the finalists came to the Morgan House in March 2000 to present their proposals.

PRESENTATIONS

Holl made an eloquent case for his bold submission. His firm had devised a number of schemes; the model he showed represented a curving L-shaped monolith in glass set within, and connecting, the three historic buildings. Judged only on its own terms—as an art object—it was dazzling. Holl said he conceptualized it as a "glowing heart." He believed that, "as a new infrastructure connecting three historic stone buildings, the new expansion would be a glowing unifier for the Morgan complex. This geometry of con-nections takes an architectural language of gentle turns, forming spaces which give free-flowing movement between the original buildings."[7] The glass curtain walls, which were to have a translucent matte finish "in complimentary contrast" to the stone buildings, were, at the same time, to link them. "Without mullions or shiny surfaces, it is an archi-tecture that whispers,"[8] he said. The new work was to have a zinc roof, as does the Annex. Holl connoted the form of his scheme with the Morgan's intellectual mission, stating, "Thoughts spiral up: The new geometry is analogous to the process of gaining knowledge—one moves forward while constantly circling the wisdom of the past."[9] A skilled watercolorist, Holl prepared renderings of the scheme's interiors that, with their

Within the section drawing:
SCHOLAR'S READING ROOM
READING ROOM STAFF
ADMINISTRATION
THAW CONSERVATION CENTER | COLLECTION SUPPORT | STAFF LOUNGE
REFERENCE STACKS
REFERENCE CATALOGING | REFERENCE STACKS
EXHIBITION GALLERIES
LOBBY
37TH STREET
AUDITORIUM
ARCHIVES
EXHIBIT STAGING AND STORAGE | MAINTAINANCE SHOP
CROSS SECTION THROUGH NEW BUILDING

Fig. 19. Steven Holl's first proposal

pleasing sketching and washes, looked as if they might have been part of a Morgan drawings exhibition (Fig. 19).

Hardy mastered the details of the program along with the existing conditions of the site and the regulatory constraints of the building envelope. Speaking with professorial authority and fluidity, he took the committee step-by-step through his scheme. Of the three finalists, he engaged the architectural history of the Morgan most deeply. In fact he turned it to daring, provocative use. Hardy pointed out that when the Morgan House was erected in the 1850s, it had been a three-story, basically square residence and that a late 1880s addition virtually doubled its size. In order to provide a cleaner footprint in which to gain more usable space, he proposed returning the house to something like its original arrangement, eliminating its back half. He proposed attaching a five-story masonry structure to its rear with "a geometric grid similar to the McKim's [and] balanced fenestration patterns that echo proportions of adjacent windows."[10] (Fig. 20) Hardy believed that the addition should respect the urban scale of Murray Hill and the Morgan environs. A new building, he thought, in massing and materials should be "compatible," especially with the McKim building. He further proposed creating a glass system that would link the addition to—and offset it from—the original library and Annex.

Fig. 20. Hugh Hardy's first scheme

Aside from the preservation issues that the proposal would set off, it provoked an internal discussion about the role of the Morgan's landmarks in the institution's current and future museum and library activities. The possibility of a more generous footprint on the north side of the site inspired enticing thoughts of less fragmented spaces for a complex that would hold an auditorium, galleries, and a new reading room. Conversely, Hardy's proposal posed unsparing preservation questions. If a building that grew or changed were to be returned to an earlier state, to which historical moment exactly? How does an institution desperate for usable space confront a building legacy that physically hems it in? How does an organization whose mission is to preserve the past appropriately respect its own history, even when its architectural legacy effectively thwarts necessary, or at least desirable, growth?

A measured, thoughtful speaker, Williams began by acknowledging the enormous challenge of expanding and changing the Morgan site in a way that would add new program space while respecting its historic fabric. He then offered two alternatives. Each honored his conceptual intention of seeing "the three landmarks set in a field of green, essentially standing as independent structures."[11] One modestly replaced the 1950s brick building with a structure of comparable size and a new central court. Because its assignable new space was modest, it would have required moving some functions off site. The other scheme, which the firm clearly preferred, was both more dramatic and, Williams admitted, would be more expensive to build. It called for a "raised and elegant strongbox, a 'reliquary' that would be cantilevered above the old buildings."[12] This elevated building, on the northeast corner of the site, would appear to be "diaphanous and subtly gilded or bronzed,"[13] a kind of "jewel box" behind a metal screen of shimmering materials (at the time, Williams brought up the possible use of gold leaf against stainless steel

and white bronze; Fig. 21). He likened these giltlike walls to the Morgan's decorated
bindings and illuminated manuscripts and the jewel box imagery to the institution's role
as a treasury of art and books. Its rectilinear form and some proportions were derived
from the McKim building and Annex. The firm had closely examined the visitor experience at the Morgan and had given some thought as to how to enhance it. Both options
admirably clarified external and internal circulation.

As the Morgan committee later discussed the proposals, it readily acknowledged
the imagination and distinction of each. In the committee's eyes, however, each had at
least one major tripping point. Holl's, along with one of Williams and Tsien's proposed
new structures, were thought to be too large and risked overpowering the McKim
building. Hardy's approach to the Morgan House was seen as clever and tempting
but untenable.

All three firms had generally fulfilled program requirements, with Hardy offering
the greatest amount of usable space. And while all were plausible, none created the level
of excitement the committee had hoped for. After weeks of further consideration of the
schemes and reflective discussion, the Morgan took the unusual step of asking the three
firms if they would participate in another round of competition.[14] However surprised,
disappointed, or frustrated they may have been at this prospect, they agreed.

COMPETITION: ROUND TWO

The Morgan soon prepared revised guidelines and goals based on the evolution in the
project as it was shaped by the competitors and its own sharpening vision. The guidelines conveyed to the respective competitors the strengths and weaknesses of their first

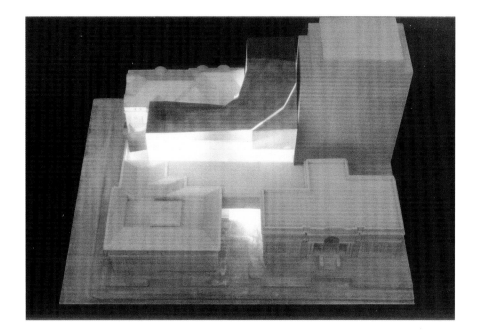

Fig. 22. Holl's revised design proposal

entries as the committee assessed them but did not disclose the competing schemes to the architects in order to maintain a level playing field.

Holl's second scheme held to the essential forms, materials, and conceits of the first entry but with the overall massing reduced and internal arrangements more developed (Fig. 22).

Hardy offered two solutions, both of which left the Morgan House intact. Moreover, one option employed it to new effect, by generally carrying over the house's style and color to a new building on the northern portion of the site (Fig. 23). For the alternate scheme, Hardy took a corporate modern approach to the new structure that sharply offset it from the landmarks (Fig. 24). With similar proportions and generous, rational internal arrangements, the two schemes were radically different stylistic solutions.

The prominent feature of Williams and Tsien's second submission was a more conventional tower. It had graceful touches characteristic of the firm's work: varied and inventively chosen facade materials, and projecting planes and asymmetric openings that articulated its simple geometry (Fig. 25).

IMPASSE

The committee met in several sessions analyzing the proposals. There was mild enthusiasm or qualified support for each scheme. Striving to chart a course that the committee as a whole might be willing to take, Parker, Charlie, and I met for most of a day and studied the proposals exhaustively. When this exercise brought us no further, Charlie queried our advisor, Paul Goldberger, as to whether an architectural search and competition of the type conducted had ever reached such an impasse. Goldberger told Charlie that he thought it was very unusual but that it had happened.

As the committee engaged in challenging sessions, and bilateral conversations inevitably took place (and before the official close of the competition), Renzo Piano's name was mentioned. In this unsettled, unsettling place, where there was no clear-cut

winner and no certainty whatsoever that Piano would actually take the commission, the competition was formally closed.

The Morgan was unaware as to whether news of the competition had reached the press, nor did it want its hard decision to reflect unflatteringly on the institution or the finalists, all of whom it regarded highly. And though it prepared for hard questions from the media, for whatever reasons, it never faced them.

ETHOS

In commissioning new architecture for the Morgan, we greatly wish to retain the style and scale of the institution. The Morgan style—or what might more accurately be called its ethos—is that almost inexpressible feeling one has as one moves through the Library. The Morgan's intimate scale must also be maintained. We thought it would be helpful to offer a few remarks on each of these matters.

THE ORIGINAL LIBRARY, THE COLLECTIONS, AND THE MORGAN ETHOS

The original Morgan library by Charles McKim is a superb example of American Beaux-Arts (or American Renaissance) architecture. Restrained on the exterior, the interior is appointed in richly colorful stones and wood and is decidedly elegant, almost baroque. It conveys grandeur, yet is not aloof or lifeless. While other buildings in the complex also derive from the classical tradition, the McKim building is its finest expression here and the institution's foremost architectural presence.

One finds similar superlative qualities in the Morgan collections, which contain the finest, rarest, and most beautiful examples in their respective fields. The presence and display of objects of such outstanding aesthetic and historic significance, along with the architectural merit of the McKim building, has been the source of the Morgan's reputation for quality and for its atmosphere—or ethos—upon which many remark with awe.

It is from the quality and character of the McKim building that new architecture should take its cues—not its American Renaissance style, per se, but its intelligence, richness, balance, and restrained elegance. New work should be equally compelling and beautiful.

RENZO PIANO

There had been, in retrospect, a prologue of great consequence to the Morgan's pursuit of Piano. Members of the selection committee were disappointed that Piano, when formally asked to offer "qualifications" as the competition began, did not submit them. At the committee's behest, we appealed to him personally. By chance, I spoke with Piano when he returned Charlie's telephone call. After I told him of our interest, Renzo said that he knew the Morgan Library and mentioned that a friend, the author Umberto Eco, often talked of its extraordinary collections. Signaling that he was aware of the Morgan's eminence, he went on to say that at this stage of his career, competitions presented hard choices, he was busy with the redevelopment of the Potsdammer Platz in Berlin and other work, and pursuing the Morgan commission was not compelling.

Piano insisted I tell Charlie and the Trustees that his unwillingness to compete was not borne of arrogance, though he did say that entering a competition "can waste a lot of time and that it was often a 'beauty contest.'" (At this point, finding his comments so unexpected and pertinent, I began taking verbatim notes.) His essential resistance, he emphasized, was not the time that competitions took but the energy. At this period in his life, Piano said, he wanted to focus both his energy and what he called, with disarming candor, his "passion" in the most productive way.

The architect proceeded, in politic phrases, to suggest that the Morgan consider dropping the competitive process altogether. "I suggest that you go to see buildings and make a decision on an architect that way. The risk of your choice is lowered by going to visit the actual buildings of possible architects. In fact, if you can, arrange both to see their buildings and visit architects in their offices." Also, he advised, "pay attention to chemistry: how do things work between architect and client?" Finally he said, "My advice is that it would be better for you to identify and seek out an architect. Also, in being selected in this way, the architect feels very honored." He told me all this in perfect Italian-inflected English. *Go see, chemistry, honored*—ideas that he wanted to stress—were given a sharp marcato.

As our conversation wound down, Renzo offered a closing valedictory: "One never knows, if for some reason things don't work out with the competition, be in touch." He wished us luck. Thanking him for his candor, I did not expect to speak with him again.

Reporting this conversation to Charlie, I added that I never had a telephone conversation with someone who had such a charming phone manner. (In time, we at the Morgan would learn that Piano's charm was legendary and we were to witness it ourselves.) But I also reported that I had no luck. Piano would not be submitting "qualifications."

Just short of a year later, in late spring 2000, Charlie sent Piano a letter that began:

Dear Mr. Piano,
I am writing on behalf of the Board of Trustees of the Morgan Library. As I believe you know, about a year ago we began a limited competition to select an architect for a capital project here and asked you to submit qualifications. You graciously declined, and Brian Regan, our Deputy Director, speaking for the Trustees and me, talked to you in the hope of persuading you to enter the competition, especially in the light of the exceptional interest that the committee had in your work. Brian reported that you explained why you did not wish to compete yet also mentioned that, if for any reason the competition did not turn out as we expected, you would be pleased to hear from us.
You are hearing from us! Loudly and hopefully!!!

It was this renewed overture that heralded the Morgan's retention of the Renzo Piano Building Workshop. In July 2000, as Charlie and I prepared to meet Renzo and his colleagues in Paris, we recast a short form of the program and refined a statement about both program goals and the institution's aspiration for new architecture. Specific new facilities were readily articulated, as they had grown out of years of discussion and planning. Drafting a statement about the Morgan's aesthetic hopes, intrinsically subjective, proved more challenging, but the discipline of expressing in language such general principles helped us and, I think, Piano and his colleagues communicate more fluently.

SCALE

The Library was initially Pierpont Morgan's private library, a historical circumstance that has shaped the institution. Scale—smaller rather than larger—figures importantly here. It has created a feeling of intimacy that is frequently cited as one of the Library's most admired qualities. One experiences it in the size of the buildings, in the size of the rooms, and most definitely in the general scale of the collection objects: drawings, books, miniatures, and manuscripts. Such relatively small rare materials also demand to be examined closely. Viewing and studying the Morgan collections is, therefore, generally the reverse of looking at impressionist or modernist art. Any new architecture must take this critical factor into account.

Writing about architecture elsewhere, another museum official has nicely expressed the result desired here as it relates to scale: "Spaces, forms, textures should maintain a harmonious simplicity and human proportion between the visitor, the building, and the art object."

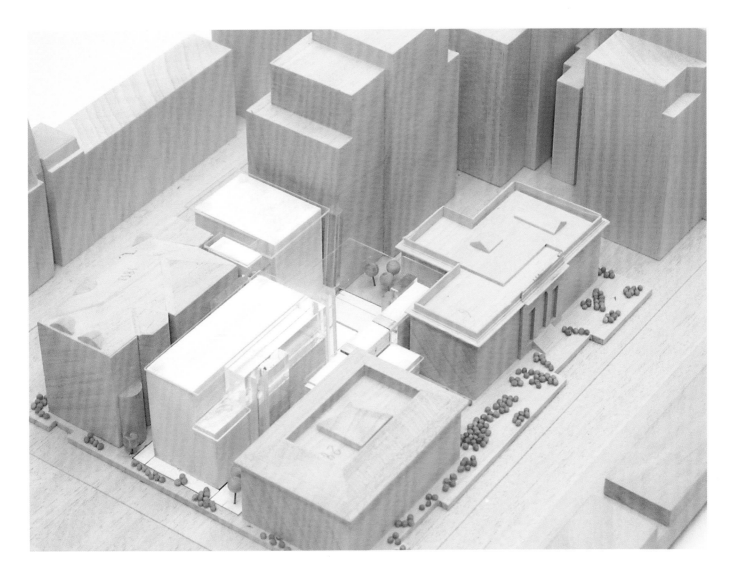

Fig. 26. A model of the Renzo Piano proposal, from above

WALKING AND WALKING AND DRAWING

Asked how he begins to design, Renzo responds that he invariably starts by walking around the site. "Walking and walking and also listening to what the site tells you—listening for its genius loci," he says.[15] Although Piano had studied photographs and plans of existing conditions, the "start by walking" method was demonstrably true for the Morgan scheme. He spent most of a September 2000 day pacing 36th and 37th Streets and up and down Madison Avenue (much of the time smoking a cigar) and touring the Morgan interior (without a cigar). That evening, he and several colleagues, including Giorgio Bianchi, who became project architect for the Morgan commission, met Charlie and a few others from the Morgan for dinner at a restaurant overlooking Madison Square Park.

As table conversation turned to the project, Renzo took out one of his signature green felt-tipped pens and started to draw on a sheet of white paper. "You have three historic buildings," he said, speaking as he drew a simple plan, marking it with *A* for the McKim building, *B* for the Annex, and *C* for the Morgan House. "All are old and we must respect them," he said. He smiled and added, "but only one is truly great." He noted that over the years other structures had been attached to them, additions that he felt had diminished the prime landmarks. He said that he wanted to free the three old buildings

of their later additions and insert within the campus three new buildings of various sizes. He drew them: *1* between the McKim building and the Annex, *2* between the Annex and the Morgan House, *3* at the back of the Morgan house, and *4* between the house and the apartment building next door on the 37th Street. He said that he thought there should be a glass-enclosed piazza or central court in the middle of the buildings and glass-enclosed spaces linking the complex. Together, they would constitute a six-building complex (plus a slender new utility and office structure attached to the back of the Morgan house; Fig. 26). Much of the newly created space was to be below ground and the new buildings (or pavilions) no higher than the historic buildings (Fig. 27). He wanted these new architectural elements to be as unobtrusive as possible and provide for many vistas—enabling those outside to see into the Morgan and those inside to be aware of the cityscape. There would have to be plenty of natural light. His plan would require removing some of the additions, including the Garden Court, that had been erected around the principal landmarks. This surgical removal, as he fashioned it, would permit all the structures to be experienced as freestanding works. He said that he particularly longed to "liberate" the McKim building.

In proposing the central glass-enclosed court, Renzo spoke about the entire scheme in ancient terms. He remarked that it should look and function like a village and that the central court might be regarded as a piazza, and, like those in the villages of his homeland, comprise a nexus of roads as well as a place where people meet for any number of purposes and pleasures. The historic rooms and exhibition galleries were to be the temples, churches, and public buildings of this scheme, while the shop, café, and the areas serving similar functions would be its profane places, as he called them. In all, it was a place in which visitors would be nourished intellectually, spiritually, and temporally.

Other metaphors would join the village conceit. The vault for the collections, Renzo said, was a treasury or a safe house, nestled in carved-out Manhattan schist and constituting an almost literal, adamantine conviction to keep the Morgan collections secure for all time. Within, he wanted to create a mysterious, storied place of seemingly unending shelves of books and manuscripts, inspired by reading a story by the Argentine novelist Jorge Luis Borges.[16] That evening Renzo also introduced other major elements of his scheme: moving the public entrance to Madison Avenue and creating a small pavilion between the McKim building and the Annex.

To an amazing degree, the essential—and most poetic—aspects of Renzo Piano's Morgan scheme were sketched out that evening. He talked about his concept to Morgan Trustees a few days later. After four months of further study, at a January 2001 Board of Trustees meeting, he formally presented what he termed a conceptual scheme, with drawings and basic models (Fig. 28). Former *New York Times* architecture critic Herbert Muschamp called Renzo Piano the "poet of circulation," and the clarity of the internal arrangements, adjacencies, and horizontal and vertical axes he offered was brilliant. When Piano finished, he left the room so that the Trustees might discuss his proposal. That discussion had an unmistakable tenor: the Morgan was in the right hands.

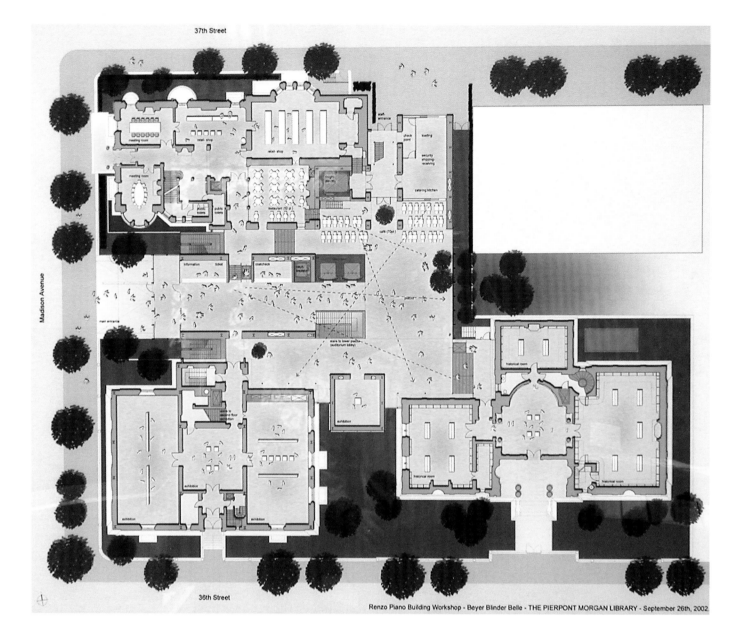

Fig. 28. A relief plan of the Piano scheme

(*Following pages*) **Fig. 29. The large exhibition model of Piano's scheme**

After a unanimous vote to retain him, Piano was called back to the room to something rarely heard in Morgan Board meetings: spontaneous applause. He told the Trustees that they would be on a long journey with him, adding that he was thrilled, honored, and humbled to join them. If one were looking for symbolic devices, a subtle one would have been seen in this gifted, genial, unpretentious man's lapel. The coveted, colorful threads of the French Légion d'Honneur wound around his buttonhole might have been taken for "Morgan red."

DESIGN REVIEW IN NEW YORK

As preparation for gaining approval from the Landmarks Preservation Commission for the project, the Morgan and its professional teams presented the Piano scheme to the preservation, architectural, and community groups who were likely to comment or testify on the project.[17] Their response could not be predicted, but after a couple of meetings, we knew that we were gaining influential supporters and advocates. The qualities that made the Piano solution persuasive translated immediately to most and eventually to virtually everyone. Sherida Paulsen, who was Landmarks Preservation Commissioner by the time the project was formally reviewed and granted a Certificate of Appropriateness, was alert and supportive, as was her successor, Robert Tierney. Partisans of the classical revival style sounded minor dissonance, presumably because they had hoped that changes to the Morgan would be rendered in their preferred architectural style. It never remotely coalesced into protest. The scheme's profound regard for the McKim building and the Annex—along with the way they were freed from intervening additions in order to be celebrated as detached pavilions—was, it seemed, manifest even to those who may have been inclined to lament the removal of the classically derived work of the McKim-Annex linking structure and the 1960s and 1970s additions.

ROUNDING OUT THE TEAM

Early in our association, Renzo Piano appointed Giorgio Bianchi project architect for the Morgan Commission. Giorgio, like Renzo, is a native of Genoa and was a 15-year veteran of the Workshop when the Morgan project began. The Piano design aesthetic is in his marrow. Beyer Blinder Belle, the New York firm selected as executive architects, had worked effectively for the Morgan during the project's planning phase. While the Morgan introduced the Piano Workshop to Beyer Blinder Belle, it was with no obligation to partner for the expansion. Among other strengths, BBB's reputation for historic preservation in New York, we thought, could help in developing solutions that the Landmarks Commission would deem acceptable. We therefore were pleased when the Renzo Piano Building Workshop and Beyer Blinder Belle, represented principally by Richard Southwick and Michael Wetstone, joined forces. Richard, seasoned and sensible, handled the firm's executive architect role with deference to Renzo but without detriment to BBB's sense of ownership or the unique resources, especially in preservation, that it brought to the table. Wetstone added estimable architectural skills and a prized virtue in planning a complex architectural venture: near perfect recall of facts, figures, and the sequence of project development. When others' memories faded or failed, he invariably retrieved the information. The RPBW-BBB team was supported by Robert Silman, a dean of New York structural engineers, and Cosentini Associates, as mechanical engineers, and a host of other specialists.

With Piano's encouragement, the Morgan engaged Andrew Klemmer and his firm, Paratus Group, to serve as its owner's representative and project manager. For five years he was the most central adviser to the Morgan. Among Paratus's first tasks was leading Morgan staff through exercises that rigorously measured and codified existing uses of the complex and clarified goals, resulting in a comprehensive program document from which the Morgan and its architects would work.

DESIGN DEVELOPMENT

There are two Renzo Piano Building Workshops, one in Genoa, Renzo Piano's home, the other in Paris, where the Morgan project was designed. The distance between New

Fig. 30. The Renzo Piano Building Workshop model shop

(*Opposite*) Fig. 31. A model showing expanded glass panels

York and Paris determined the character and rhythm of the exchange between the Morgan and the Piano Workshop. After a few planning sessions, ground rules emerged. The Morgan was called upon to offer program requirements and could even modify them. We could comment on design, but we were gently discouraged from offering specific solutions. During design development, we met about every other month in sessions of several days, occasionally in New York, usually in Paris. The gap between meetings— and the Piano Workshop's desire to fully develop design ideas before showing them to the Morgan—meant only reasonably mature solutions were presented. Though it led to some dead ends, for the most part it was a productive modus operandi (Fig. 29).

CHOICE OF BUILDING MATERIAL

Once the parti of the new work was set, Piano turned to the exterior building material. He expressed early on that it was "quite an interesting idea to use a material found on the site—this gives us stone, copper, and bronze." He pointed to the door and window casements and the fence surrounding the site. "Copper becomes bronze-colored. Copper may be the most interesting. Bronze, I fear, in these proportions, would lose joy. And architecture must have a sense of joy."

As for the landmarked structures providing the cue for the building materials— marble in the case of the McKim building and Annex and brownstone for the Morgan House—of the new work, Renzo's response was sharp and rational: "Stone would have the effect of destroying the scheme." He insisted that "Stone is structural not cladding.

And steel is the structure of this scheme." He cited the Morgan's historic architecture as support. "Look at the McKim building. Marble is the structure and marble is the material you see. Marble was right then." At this, he shifted into lecture mode. "Let's talk about modernity. This project we are creating is of our time. It should reflect it. We're not building a stone structure. The structure is of metal. It is steel." He hastened to add that steel would impart a comparable sense of strength and stability to the marble of the McKim building and Annex. And he thought that strength and stability, in the metaphoric sense, should be associated with an institution that preserves fragile materials of artistic and cultural importance.

From the start, glass was also an essential material in Renzo's plan for the Morgan. The interstices of glass between the buildings vested the scheme with a literal and figurative lightness (Fig. 31). Further, glass, set in three-foot-wide steel panels constituted the walls and roof of the interior piazza, carrying over, in a different manner, the former garden court. There were, however, practical considerations. Glass must be cleaned. In New York, it must be cleaned often, and cleaning acres of it in midtown Manhattan would be an additional operating expense.

When Charlie expressed misgivings about steel as a facade material and asked Piano to consider something else, Renzo briefly considered a steel structural system with infill panels of stucco. He quickly concluded, however, that, "stucco does not have a lot of dignity in the United States. In Venice it's dignified, but not in America." Nor is it a practical material in our climate. During this volley over building materials, Renzo good-naturedly said, "I'm very pleased about being challenged. To challenge each other is good." And he came to believe that "plain steel may be too rude, too primitive."

MADISON AVENUE FACADE

Choices for the Madison Avenue pavilion's facade brought the most challenging, protracted aspect of design development. Given that a steel-paneled grid formed the overall building system, these panels were also the logical material and pattern for the facade of the Madison Avenue pavilion. But Charlie pressed Renzo several times on whether the steel panels, as the public face of the renovated Morgan, might appear insufficiently warm and welcoming and "too massive and inelegant."

These misgivings were reconveyed at the first of a three-day series of design development sessions in 2002 at the Paris Workshop. The following morning, Renzo entered our meeting smiling, shaking an index finger in the air, exclaiming, "I have an idea! I have an idea!" He proposed that the grid system be carried down to street level and paneled in glass. (The current design had called for the two upper stories to be projected above, or cantilevered over, the entrance.) Although this change would, he believed, make the structure appear less like the "floating box" that he had described earlier, the pavilion would engage the street more hospitably (Figs. 32 and 33). It seemed to all of us an appealing urbanistic gesture that had the practical result of forming an enclosed vestibule.

The Workshop developed a series of alternative approaches to the western facade.

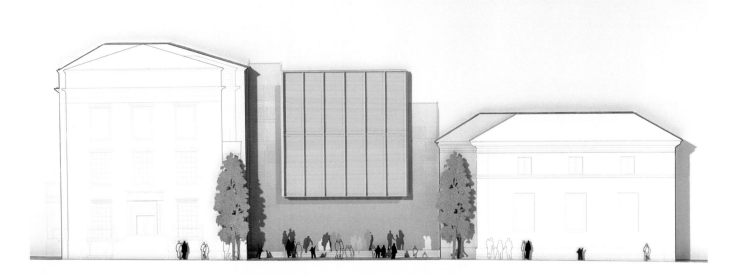

Fig. 32. A drawing of the floating box

Fig. 33. A model of the facade extended downward, creating a vestibule

One replaced the opaque steel panels with glass. In addition to relieving the field of steel, such visual disclosure to the outside world was symbolic of the further institutional "opening up" that the project represented. But this glass facade ran counter to the function of the spaces behind it: the reading room and a large new gallery. The display or use of the Morgan's works on paper in these areas demanded, for incontrovertible conservation reasons, low interior light levels. In response, the Workshop experimented with steel panels (over a glass-paneled facade) that opened and closed like giant vertical louvers, adjusted by a photosensor as exterior light conditions changed (Fig. 34).[18]

The persistent concern about the appearance of the Madison Avenue facade also induced Piano's team to transpose the entire panelized grid system from a six-foot to a three-foot module and minimize its horizontal members. Some saw this greater division of units as creating a more emphatic vertical emphasis and visual lightening of the massing. Others thought it compromised the ineffably beautiful geometry of Renzo's first scheme.[19] At one point during this debate (and as he had once or twice before) Parker

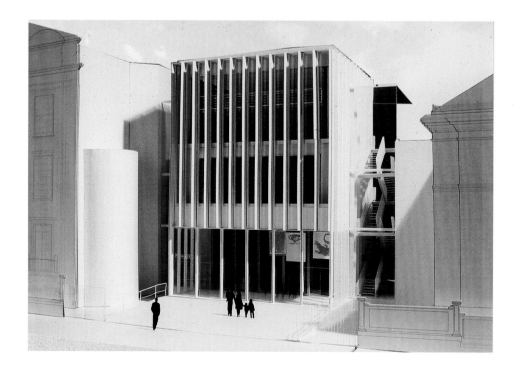

urged that we "let Renzo be Renzo"—reminding everyone of the institution's desire for artistic vision. These design development byways led to important breakthroughs (such as the glass-enclosed vestibule), several blind alleys, or, as in the case of the Madison Avenue facade, a circumnavigation to a design feature originally preferred by Renzo and validated by experimentation.

COLOR

The decision to paint or coat the steel implied a choice of color. With stone or untreated metal, choice is ostensibly limited by colors occurring naturally in such materials. Painted surfaces permit virtually limitless choices. And with that, the Morgan project team was offered another reminder that seldom do many choices accelerate decision making.

Renzo was initially drawn to a range of greens, corresponding with the coppers and bronze found on the site. The Workshop went on to explore bolder colors, experimenting with painting each of the three pavilions in a different color: red, green, and ochre. Some liked this for the manner in which it articulated the three structures, visually reduced the massing of the new work, and permitted each of the pavilions to respond to the distinct streetscapes they faced. Others saw unsympathetic precedent in the Pompidou Centre's polychrome. Charlie emphatically rejected the idea, to the unspoken relief of his colleagues. Even Renzo, during a discussion about a different palette, admitted that, "Well, we probably won't do this, but it is an interesting possibility that tells us something about what we are searching for." During one such session, when we seemed to be going in circles over the Madison Avenue facade and the color of the steel, he assured us, "Don't panic. I've been in this place twenty-five times before. It always comes out right, though we don't yet see the solution."

"Off-white" for the entire steel system was a refrain in client-architect conversations for well over two years, and it became insistently more appealing. Adding the slightest amount of pink or rose would provide a subtle correspondence to the Tennessee pink marble of the McKim building and Annex. In the end off-white with a pink cast was chosen not only for its unself-conscious novelty but also because it would blend best with the mix of building materials and colors in and around the Morgan site. Piano maintained that, "We have to get a color that is not trying to be new. And it must not be too heavy. It must give joy." For some of us, part of its "joy" sprang from the sheer relief, after exchanges that were by turns stimulating and enervating, of settling upon a generally satisfactory choice.

Charlie reviewed color mock-ups at the Genoa Workshop in March 2004. He gave provisional approval, contingent upon how they would look—not only tinged by the Mediterranean sun but in their urban setting. The following month, on a bright spring day, a group from the Morgan approved the choice. A group of Building Committee members reviewed the mock-ups erected in front of the Madison Avenue side of the Annex. Eventually we were frank with each other and acknowledged that the proposed color would be perceived as off-white and the pink hue was successful but subtle. Trustee Charles F. Morgan, descended from the founders and with an encyclopedic knowledge of the institution's buildings, likened the color to the Tennessee pink marble of the McKim building and Annex, adding that "in wet weather, you really see why it's called Tennessee pink!"

Richard Menschel, a building committee member especially attuned to a modernist aesthetic, liked the color. But he also thought that at this point it should be left in Piano's hands. "This is why," Menschel commented, "you hire someone like Renzo." Annette de la Renta saw the samples later and registered her reaction. Committee members had particular confidence in Mrs. de la Renta's eye and listened attentively to her nuanced views. She, too, was pleased by the proposed color and, in entirely separate conversations, her words were an almost perfect echo of Richard Menschel's.

Renzo came to see the color mock-ups at the site when he was next in New York. Standing near the western corner of Madison Avenue and 36th Street and judging the samples positioned in front of the Annex, he said his preference was confirmed. Sweeping his eyes from south to north, he then remarked on the palette of red and brown along with lighter masonry in the buildings along Madison Avenue. He said he thought the proposed color would be at home among Madison Avenue's *allée* of colors. Renzo then began to enact a pontifical benediction. Waving an imaginary aspergilium, he pronounced, "I bless this color." The Morgan staff and Trustees and the Landmarks Preservation Commission would each give their own endorsement—albeit with less panache.

INTERIOR DESIGN AND FINISHES: PHILOSOPHY AND PRACTICE

The philosophy that informed the exterior of the complex, "allowing the old to remain old and the new work to be of today," as Renzo expressed it, was brought to the table again as we began talking about the appearance of interior spaces. Though we had heard his thoughts on the matter before, and they were familiar words and ideas, Renzo is never reluctant to explain and repeat his reasoning. As interior design development began, we knew what he wanted.

But Charlie took the lead, too, and we prepared a letter reiterating that the extant interiors (their warmth and scale, not their precise style) should provide the clue to the new work. Agreeing, Renzo noted, "The last century was about hands doing beautiful work. It is not necessarily that way today, but all our choices must convey quality and elegance." We agreed upon contemporary design and materials, as long as they conveyed "refinement and elegance." Early proposals for stair systems and rails, for instance, were found too industrial for persuasive use in the Morgan, and the Piano team quickly offered alternatives. When there were similar concerns about lighting fixtures, especially the *perroquet* light, developed by the Workshop with the Italian manufacturer iGuzzini, we worked together to find visually quieting solutions.

The new, paneled interiors—particularly the entry and auditorium—called for considerable use of cherrywood.[20] Renzo preferred that the new woodwork be lighter than the old. The Workshop was at first inclined to a hue that was more orange than we liked. We quickly agreed on a level of color saturation for the stain; a later variant with more brown (that also seemed to us harmonious with the totality of wood finishes throughout the complex) proved mutually agreeable.

Having anticipated that marble, stone, or terrazzo floors would be consistent with the small monumentality of the place and most sensible in terms of longevity and upkeep, we were surprised when Renzo proposed wood flooring for the major public spaces. He persuaded us, however, that wood would be visually warmer, easier on the visitors' feet, and extremely durable. Together we selected plain-sawn oak flooring.

GALLERIES

Exhibitions, at the core of a museum's purpose, present unique challenges to an institution such as the Morgan, whose collections are primarily composed on paper or vellum. Three months is the normative period for displaying such fragile, light-sensitive materials. Longer exposure, even in controlled environments, risks deterioration. This means that larger numbers of drawings, manuscripts, and books can be displayed in the future, but, as in the past, they cannot be exhibited for long periods, which prohibits having any single object on permanent display. Exhibiting the Morgan's permanent collection thus brings challenges not faced by most art museums.

CUBE

Forming an architectonic hyphen between the McKim building and the Annex, the south pavilion became smaller during design development; and within it was planned a space that formed a perfect cube, "six meters by six meters by six meters" as Piano often repeated (Fig. 35). It was inspired, he said, by Renaissance *studioli* he had encountered in Italy that were perfect cubes. They remained fixed in his imagination, and he dreamed of creating a modern interpretation of one for the Morgan. But not everyone at the

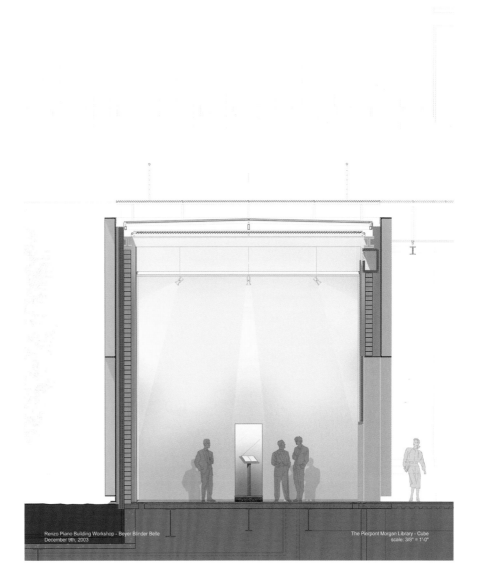

Morgan was initially won over. Some thought that this pavilion would detract from east-looking views of the original library. Piano's response was to recess it deeper into the piazza, further deferring to the McKim building and saving a larger swath of garden. This also made the pavilion more prominent from interior perspectives.

Defying the axiom that form follows function, the smallest pavilion did not immediately find a purpose. The Morgan considered various uses for it: a visitors' center, an interactive education center, or a gallery for a sampling of the collections, illuminated manuscripts, or great drawings. The uncertainty of how to employ this space optimally was offset by a growing enthusiasm for its perfect proportions, intimate lines, and the filtered natural light from the ceiling, all of which might give it the character of a *tempietta* or chapel. As ideas for the cube's use were considered, the Morgan decided that, at least upon reopening, a selection of decorative arts treasures would be exhibited there. This seemed, in retrospect, an inevitable purpose for the space, perfect in every way. So, well before construction began, form and function, did, in fact, align. Not only was the Morgan won over by Renzo's cube and its purpose, there was the gratification of naming this gallery for Clare Eddy Thaw.[21]

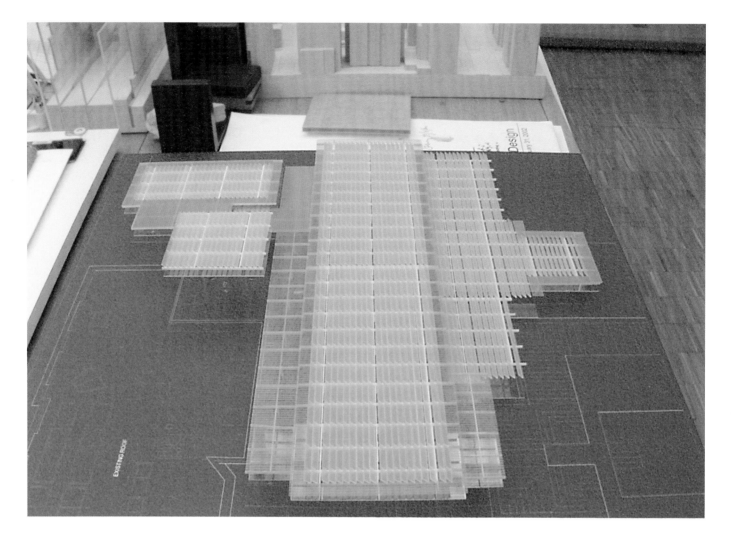

Fig. 36. A model of the roof structure

"LYRICAL" NATURAL LIGHT

During the discussion about the light-filtering roof structures of the cube and the reading room, some Morgan participants wondered whether such a complex system, with layers of movable baffles and screens, was sensible (Fig. 36). Were we justified in installing and operating a system that would be calibrated to block rather than permit natural light? Was the effect too subtle? Could electric lighting prove to be of equal or comparable quality? This probing struck a nerve in Renzo. "There is a beauty, complexity, poetry in having natural light coming from above—natural light is lyrical." He had no doubt about its importance to the cube gallery.

Renzo would say, I think, that he led us to perceive the "lyrical" quality of natural light. For our part, we helped him to appreciate more fully the nature, scale, beauty, and delicacy of the Morgan's collections when curators staged for him what Charlie termed a "Bartholomew's Fair"—a presentation of a variety of objects in the collections.[22]

Examining examples of the greatest treasures of civilization is invariably thrilling in such private sessions, and for Renzo, it registered powerfully. The two-laned road of client-architect and architect-client exchange was thus widened, allowing a deeper dialogue and making new architecture for the Morgan a more informed collaboration.

It was readily agreed that the new galleries, cube, and second floor of the Madison

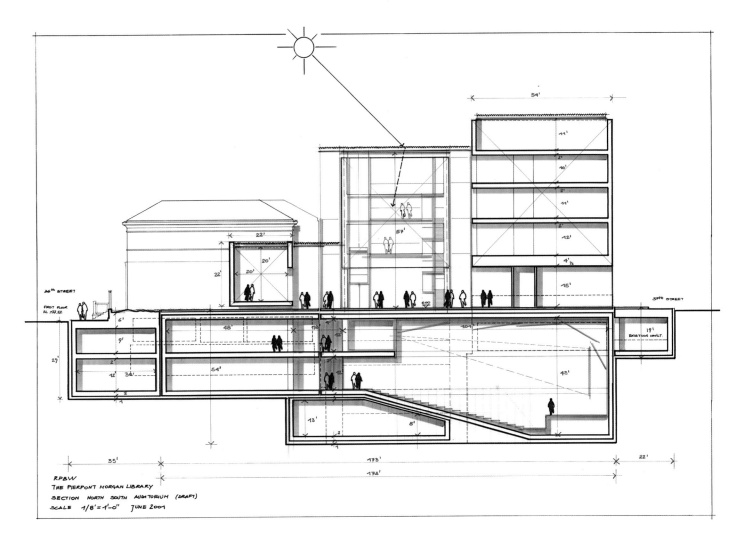

RPBW
THE PIERPONT MORGAN LIBRARY
SECTION NORTH SOUTH AUDITORIUM (DRAFT)
SCALE 1/8'=1'-0" JUNE 2001

Fig. 37. A section drawing showing various grade levels

(*Following pages*) **Fig. 38. A model of Gilder Lehrman Hall**

Avenue pavilion would be in a modern aesthetic. The decision, made in an early planning phase, to assign some galleries exclusively to a single collection was reversed when tested by the exercise of laying out future exhibitions. In the end, curators asked for maximum installation flexibility. A New York specialty firm was retained to develop exhibition case work in collaboration with the Piano Workshop and Morgan staff.[23]

The former reading room was converted into a gallery, creating an exhibition suite on the first floor of the Annex. This decision again triggered philosophical and practical questions about the renovation and rehabilitation of extant spaces.[24] We briefly entertained commemorating the room's time-honored history by preserving its fixtures (the bookcases, gallery, and select furniture). The more realistically we projected how exhibitions would be installed there, however, we came to realize that these features would become impediments to the space's new function. Charlie particularly felt that reverence rather than respect for the past would make us beholden to history. And Giorgio cautioned that carrying over old fixtures in this gallery could make the space, in a memorable colloquialism, *non carne non pesce*— "neither meat nor fish." We were persuaded by Renzo and Giorgio to bring the two rooms into balance, with the fabric walls, low wainscoting, and parquet floor of the exhibition room setting the tone for the rehabilitated former reading room.[25]

HALL

Although many aspects of Renzo Piano's architecture claimed the attention of the Morgan selection committee, auditoriums in Lyon and Turin were especially appealing —both to the eye and ear. Spare, rectilinear rooms composed of fine woods, vibrant, monochromatic seats, and acoustical devices (also inherently decorative), these halls are stunning examples of the Piano aesthetic. We wanted such a space at the Morgan that could serve equally well as a concert venue for its respected music programs and an auditorium for lectures and other programs.[26] We knew that these multiple functions engendered a challenging assignment: making a space in which the spoken word would be intelligible yet sufficiently resonant for music.

The relatively large cubic dimensions of the hall made situating it underground a logical choice once extensive excavation had been deemed essential (Fig. 37). Several locations were tested but only one, at the northeast corner of the site, offered sufficient space and the correct adjacencies for safety code (egress) compliance. While an auditorium with seating for 350 to 400 had been discussed in the blue-sky days of planning, the envelope for the hall became an exigency that the team worked to optimize (Fig. 38). It led to plans for three stage sizes, with a range of 239 to 290 seats. The option of shrinking seat size to increase capacity had no advocates.

READING ROOM

A new or substantially altered reading room for the Morgan's research function was a prime motivation of the project. This program element also immediately struck Renzo's fancy, with great historic precedents beguiling him: Michelangelo's Laurentian Library in Florence, the fabled reading room of the British Library, Labrouste's seminal Bibliothèque Sainte-Genevieve and his later Bibliothèque impériale (nationale), both in Paris. In his early visits to the Morgan, Piano also observed that the reading room, through length of service and familiarity, had acquired a patina and venerable character that he thought should be honored. He loved the warmth of its wood as well as its enveloping bookcases and wanted to carry over these elements, along with the gallery, to his plan.

The Morgan's new Sherman Fairchild Reading Room was a piece of the interior puzzle that fell swiftly into place. Locating it atop the Madison Avenue pavilion meant that it would be on a vertical circulation axis with the vault below and could be naturally lit through a roof structure of baffles and a screen of what the Piano team called vellum.[27] This translucent roof structure meant that Morgan holdings could be examined in natural light, matchless conditions for studying drawings, illuminated manuscripts, printed books, and other precious objects.

The requirements for the reading room's furnishings and equipment were precisely prescribed, originating with the Morgan's library professionals and the analysis and forward-thinking recommendations of Mark Dimunation of the Library of Congress, to whom the Morgan turned for advice in the early planning phase. Nonetheless there were challenges. Adding the tools of modern research (copy machines, microfilm and

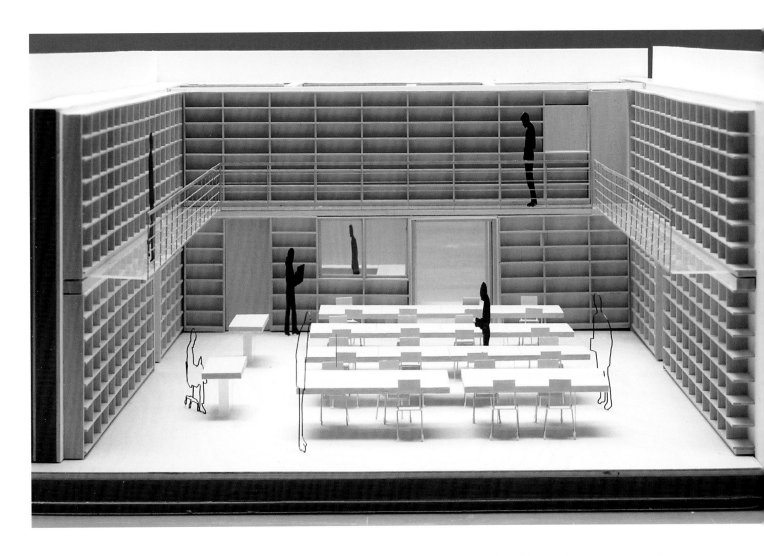

Fig. 39. A model of the Sherman Fairchild Reading Room

microfiche readers, computer work stations, and the like) to the room cluttered the expansive volume Piano first envisioned. He personally initiated changes that simplified the design, and the architectural team, along with the Morgan staff, rallied to his cause (Fig. 39).

MORGAN HOUSE DINING ROOM AND THE MORGAN SHOP

Some of the Morgan House's first floor was also given new purpose. One irresistible change was situating a restaurant in the former Morgan family dining room. In this grand domestic setting, with its Carrara and Botticino marble fireplace and wonderful frieze of gamboling, bacchic putti, visitors would be served where Morgans, Satterlees, and Pennoyers once dined (Fig. 40). Architectural decisions related to the relocated shop, however, were less apparent. When it was assigned to adjacent rooms, we again faced the preservation / renovation conundrum. Adapting the larger room as a retail area was readily achieved. Despite a high-relief cornice, a bay window, and elaborate door and window surrounds, it had ample unadorned wall surfaces. But the smaller room, with wood paneling, gilded moldings, fireplace, and chandelier, was a different matter. The architects wanted to remove these features and bring the room into stylistic conformity with the larger room. Some of us stiffened at the prospect of losing the Morgan family-era decorative scheme. Those leading retail operations understandably argued for

Fig. 40. The Morgan Dining Room

whatever approach would help, or at least not handicap, sales. Eventually it was decided that saving the room's historic appointments and creating serviceable retail space were not mutually exclusive. Most came to see that there was virtue in allowing the two wings of the shop to complement each other. It did, however, entail widening the door openings and strategic placement of the cashier's desk and gift and book display (Fig. 41).

TESTED AND SUSTAINED

The Morgan project survived two potentially debilitating traumas. The failed competition severely tested all of those involved. But the doubts that it provoked had receded fully after about a year of working with Renzo Piano. By summer 2001, the project had hit its natural rhythm. Client and architect exchanged ideas, and the Morgan and Workshop were both working toward program and design choices, Morgan Trustees were consulted on important decisions, and the machinery of official approvals moved apace. Resuming sessions after the obligatory quiet of the European August, the Morgan administrative team was scheduled to meet with Renzo and Giorgio in New York on the second Tuesday in September. The date was September 11.

The meeting with Renzo and Giorgio, of course, was postponed. They were in New York, staying in hotels on the East Side, and like everyone, stepped with trepidation

Fig. 41. The Morgan Shop

through the rest of that day and night. They came to the Morgan the following afternoon. It was a sober occasion. Renzo, usually loquacious, was muted. Charlie, famous for pushing initiatives forward and coaxing others to take, at the very least, small next steps, paused. Eventually, "post–September 11" and "after 9/11" entered our lexicon, but on the day after that fateful Tuesday, any hint of the future was hidden. By the end of our session, Renzo talked gently about the importance, in the face of catastrophic destruction, of affirming those things about which we care most, of acts that preserve and extend rather than destroy civilization. He quietly went on to say that he felt it was more important than ever for the Morgan project to continue. Charlie echoed Renzo's hope. Giorgio Bianchi and I listened in silent assent. Outside, New York's atmosphere was broken and vulnerable; yet within the protected precincts of the Morgan, this imperative seemed both plausible and necessary. During that exchange, Renzo did not have to say (because we did) that the decision to locate the vault deep in Manhattan schist seemed prescient. He sometimes referred to the vault as a "safe." The attacks of 9/11 conferred upon the word a strange, regretful meaning.

THE BOARD'S CONVICTION

In the ensuing months, Charlie and Parker along with other Trustees, though cautious about the possible economic aftermath of the terrorist attacks and the burst of the stock market technology bubble, never let the project idle. Their sense of purpose, applauded by New York City officials, helped ease the ongoing review by the Landmarks Preservation Commission.

The Trustees' conviction emanated from the board president. Parker Gilbert, in many respects, embodies, for this generation, the Morgan financial legacy. Family ties connected him to the highest reaches of the Morgan firms during the twentieth century, and he led Morgan Stanley during its metamorphosis from a privately held investment bank to a public company. Steeped in Morgan banking traditions, he assumed leadership of the most important of the Morgan philanthropic legacies and since 1988 has kept a guiding hand on the major levers of the institution. With a banker's attention to careful planning, and a financier's bias for growth, Parker at various times restrained or pushed, stood back or directed, with an instinct that few would question. The expansion project would not have begun without his interest and support, nor would it have continued without his directive to keep it moving, as milestones and crossroads were reached, especially the grievous one brought about by 9/11.

DIGGING DOWN AND BUILDING UP

F. J. Sciame was construction manager for the project. Frank Sciame, the company's eponymous founder, instilled it with a voracious dedication to quality. The Sciame team, led by Joseph Mizzi, was determined from the start to leave behind a fine building. One of Sciame's first tasks was to oversee excavation. But not a sliver of Manhattan schist could be removed until every collection item had been moved and safely stored and the entire staff, except for a small security detail, had decamped from the Morgan Library as we had known it. When Renzo first declared to Charlie that carrying out his plan would make it virtually obligatory for the entire site to be vacated, we said little but gave each other a look that said, "That'll be the day." And in the ensuing months we explored every conceivable way to keep some part of the Morgan functioning for visitors and staff. Eventually, the logic of faster, safer construction overtook that conviction. The McKim building, set up as a giant collection vault, with protected, ceiling-high metal shelving, housed not quite half the collections. Most of the other holdings were transported to a larger former bank vault at Fifth Avenue and 44th Street, where the Reader Services staff and curators were able to sustain a basic level of collection access.[28] We leased temporary quarters for the staff at this and another midtown-Manhattan location.

Beginning in summer 2003, over 46,000 tons of rock, in 1,312 truckloads, was removed (Figs. 42 and 43). The foundations of the three landmarks were secured—in some cases, pinned—and the foundation for the new construction prepared.[29] The steel infrastructure was largely completed a year later.

Fig. 44. Marble from the vein used to construct the original library and Annex

Fig. 45. Masonry restoration on the original library

(*Following pages*) Fig. 46. Below-grade construction, facing east toward the future Gilder Lehrman Hall (lower left) and lobby (center)

TOPPING OFF

The topping off ceremony, observed when the highest point of construction is reached, was held on September 14, 2004. In a building-trades tradition, prior to the ceremony, a small evergreen had been hoisted atop the crossbeam of the piazza's east roof. After an informal, plein-air lunch, Charlie thanked the workers, architects, consultants, Morgan staff, and a handful of patrons who had gathered on the northern side of the site for having brought the project to this point. September 14 also marked Charlie's eighteenth anniversary as director and Renzo's sixty-seventh birthday. Another step forward was the positioning of one of the completed painted steel panels, fabricated by the German company Gundelfingen, on the Madison Avenue facade. There was general satisfaction with the color and its consonance with the ambient buildings and neighborhood.

MARBLE RESTORATION

In 1928, when the Annex was built, the link that connected it to the McKim building was attached to the rear of the latter. Because this masonry arm was being removed, the back of the McKim building would be visible once more; in fact, it would be a prominent feature of the new interior court. This meant that a portion of the original Tennessee marble blocks in the northwest corner of the building had to be replaced. Beyer Blinder Belle, drawing upon its historic restoration expertise, replaced them "in kind" with marble from the same vein (though not the same quarry) as that used to build the 1906 and 1928 structures (Fig. 44). Overseen by Frank Prial of Beyer Blinder Belle, masons recreated the virtually mortarless "dry-laid" system that Charles McKim specified for Pierpont Morgan's library a century before (Fig. 45).[30]

BROWNSTONE BLUES

The restoration of the Morgan House "brownstone" was another matter. *Brownstone* is the common name for the sandstone used ubiquitously in New York during the second half of the nineteenth century, most of it quarried in northeastern New Jersey and central Connecticut. This soft, sedimentary stone is easily removed from the ground and responds pliantly to the saw, hammer, and chisel—qualities that made it popular with quarrymen and masons at that time. These same characteristics made it a compromised building material, made worse by a frequent practice of laying it, not in the natural bed in which it had developed over geological ages, but on its side. This created a more uniform face. It also made for a fatal flaw. Exposed to the elements, and vulnerable to freeze-thaw cycles, within decades sandstone typically begins to delaminate, shedding in vertical layers, each loss permitting further deterioration. In the case of the Morgan House, its worsening condition led the Lutheran Church, like many owners of brownstone buildings, to coat it with stucco.[31] Over the years, this covering was given layers of brown paint. Charlie often said that by the 1990s the house looked as if it had been dipped in a vat of dark chocolate.

Plans for the treatment of the house shifted during the project. Moreover the budget for it was trimmed in an early cost-reduction effort when the team thought, perhaps naively, that it would be satisfactory simply to paint the house a color that approximated the original stone, which was lighter and redder than the lugubrious brown in which it was coated.[32] In retrospect, these measures belied a pardonable ambivalence. We were like a family that resisted intervening on behalf of a somewhat dysfunctional, uncertainly loved elderly relative. In the case of the Morgan House, much of the dysfunction stemmed from two problems. Its face was constructed with intrinsically poor material. And using a building for a purpose other than the one for which it was designed (in this instance, a residence) always gives rise to concessions.

As construction advanced on the Piano project, it became apparent how prominent the Morgan House would be, especially from vantages on Madison Avenue and at the new entry. Prompted in part by this realization, we came to think that the stucco should be removed, the surviving stone stabilized or repaired, and losses patched with new stucco.[33] Following this plan, in early 2005 workers began removing the stucco. The word from 37th Street went from concern to alarm as the condition of the stone was exposed. It ranged from poor to execrable. We anticipated a low ratio of stucco to real stone. And it was indeed: less than 10 percent of the stone was in restorable condition. Among the salvageable parts were select decorative elements: lintels, surrounds, cornices, columns, pilasters, and capitals. The only reasonable action, however, was to cover the walls with the type of stucco that now coats the greatest share of New York's brownstone buildings and employ reconstituted stone for other elements.

With that decision made, and the additional cost conceded by the Trustees, Charlie pressed to make the house look as beautiful as possible, allowing it to stand confidently on its own terms among the new buildings and cleaned landmarks around it. Within the spectrum that approximated the color of the original stone, the lightest hue was chosen. That selection, while not as protracted as picking an off-white for the steel, brought patience-testing iterations of samples, mock-ups, and review. Then the actual application of the material proved both challenging and dilatory—and still beyond the upwardly

revised estimate. In the end, though, the house stood proud among the other structures, and its first floor rooms looked more charming than they had in years.

ONGOING DESIGN

In this phase we addressed how and where the institution's name would be represented at the entrance. The Workshop did not want to place the name anywhere on the Madison Avenue facade, ostensibly to preserve the purity of the grid system. Concerned about this obvious lack of public identification, Charlie and the Morgan team nonetheless accepted that we would wait and see how the facade appeared when actually built before deciding on a location for this signage, reserving the right to put it on the facade or over the main doors if another compelling position was not found. Working with the graphic design firm Pentagram and the Workshop, we eventually agreed that the formal name, The Pierpont Morgan Library, should flank the main entrance on panels constructed in the same syntax as Piano's grid system.[34]

Deliberation about furniture for the new facilities continued through much of 2005 and into 2006. Some of it was designed by the Workshop, some selected from commercial lines; in all cases there was an effort to select tables, chairs, and appointments that would look at home in the new spaces and to maintain aesthetic coherence. The Workshop took the lead with these choices, with the Morgan weighing in.[35]

LANDSCAPING

At the outset, the Morgan imagined that the site's existing landscaping would be little changed. If anything, a more traditional English garden approach was contemplated; we especially admired the ornamental planting around the New York Public Library and Bryant Park on 42nd Street. Although the Workshop arranged for a landscape designer for the project, it was soon obvious that Renzo himself had a determined vision for what landscaping would be pleasing for the site as he reimagined it.[36] He believed that all the buildings should be free from obstructing planting, rising on a lawn "like the Duomo in Pisa," as he put it. Renzo instructed that birches be planted in the gaps between the buildings so that they would be visible from outside and inside the Morgan. He also called for a line of bamboo beyond the court's eastern glass wall, providing a broad green living terminus to this magnetic east-west axis. The *Ficus benjamina* for the interior court were the subject of a minor drama. Those originally tagged for the Morgan were growing nicely in Florida until late in the summer before reopening, when they perished during a violent hurricane season. With weeks and months passing, the search for their replacements failed and there was a mad, maddening scamper to find temporary replacements in time for reopening. We settled for skimpier specimens than those selected earlier until healthier trees could be transplanted.

Fig. 47. The construction site from Madison Avenue, 2004

COMPLETION

Construction had moved along during the first months of 2005 at such a rate that an April 2006 formal opening was announced in April 2005. But the pace slackened, and by summer 2005, when the collections were due to be transferred to the new vault and the staff set to return shortly thereafter, those deadlines were missed, casualties of construction delays whose origins and their accounts had dozens of authors (Fig. 46). The collection move occurred in the late fall. When the staff ultimately returned to the campus in December 2005, it was still an active construction site, interior finishes were still under way, and new mechanical systems were being tested (Fig. 47). By January 2006, experienced hands predicted that some form of work would continue until the day of the celebratory dinner. They were right. The central court's wood flooring, put down in stages throughout the early months of 2006 and the exterior restoration of the Morgan House, moving at a glacial rate despite a mercifully mild winter, were obvious activities among many less visible ones. Teams of electricians, masonry restorers, and mechanical and elevator technicians labored straight through to the opening, leaving from the 37th Street door only hours before Parker and Gail Gilbert and Charlie and Barbara Pierce welcomed Trustees and donors in the sparkling new lobby on Madison Avenue early on the evening of April 25, 2006, and to thank them for their generosity. Support for the $102 million project, which included an endowment campaign, had come mostly from individuals. Trustees contributed well over half of the cost, and J.P. Morgan Chase and Morgan Stanley, the firms most directly descended from the founders' financial house, made substantial grants, as did several foundations. The City of New York provided its first-ever capital funding to the Morgan.

PARVIS

The generous plazalike area fronting the lobby on Madison Avenue where the Gilberts and Pierces stood had already provided an unanticipated delight. During the planning phase, we were so absorbed in considering what the Morgan would look like from the sidewalk and the street that we had not imagined what it would be like to look *out* from the Morgan. And looking out from the entry, visitors take in an enchanting urban vista. The foreground of birches and ivy leads to sweeping views from south to north along Madison Avenue: a large Beaux-Arts–derived office building, a vernacular nineteenth-century brick building, the gracious John Murray House, and an art deco structure with abundant Gothic decoration. Piercing the sky above them are the Empire State Building's finial-like antenna and a Michael Graves–designed polychrome residential tower on Fifth Avenue. This visual engagement of the city and vice versa, essential to Piano's scheme and synchronous with the Morgan's mission of reaching out to, and welcoming in, the broader public, was expressed here as well, in especially poetic terms.

Late one bright afternoon before completion, Charlie and I were standing at the future public entry. I asked him if he knew the term *parvis,* from medieval architecture.

Fig. 48. The completed Madison Avenue entrance

Never distant from his life as a professor of English literature, Charlie said yes, remembering that Chaucer used it several times in *The Canterbury Tales*. A parvis is an enclosed or semienclosed area in front of the entrance to a building, a protected yet open and embracing architectural device (Fig. 48). The Morgan's new entry seemed very much like that: a generous parvis for visitors to enter an open public space in a city in which it is scarce.

Surveying the scene and turning back to the entry, Charlie offered that, "In all, I'm confident that it's not only going to look beautiful, it's going to function magnificently."

1. Quotations of participants in the Morgan Library–Renzo Piano Building Workshop project are from the author's notes and a personal journal that was begun with the design development phase.

2. The projects included the acquisition and renovation of the Morgan House, the construction of the connecting Garden Court, the overhaul of the McKim building and the Annex climate control systems, and the creation of a large new vault, a Drawings Study Center in the Annex, and the Thaw Conservation Center on the fourth floor of the Morgan House.

3. The director appointed an internal planning committee to discuss and direct matters related to the project. He headed the committee, and Brian Regan, deputy director, served as coordinator. Other members were Margaret Holben Ellis, director of the Thaw Conservation Center, Robert Parks, director of Library and Museum Services, and Kristina W. Stillman, director of Finance and Administration. Martin Cavanaugh, director of Operations, was a member of the committee until his retirement in 2003; he was succeeded by Thomas Shannon, director of Facilities. Joan Darragh, an executive at the Brooklyn Museum of Art and coauthor of *Museum Design,* was an advisor during the early planning phase.

4. During this period, the Morgan also began a two-year process of retaining the phalanx of consultants and technical advisors that are a virtual necessity to guide and support public or private institutions through major construction in Manhattan. They were, among others, library and museum specialists, land-use and preservation counselors, zoning and building code consultants, and traffic and environmental specialists.

5. Alterations to the Morgan House fourth floor and roof, necessary for the creation of the Thaw Conservation Center, were made in the early planning stage of the larger building project and were thus subject to informal review by the commission. This engendered an exchange among the participants that ultimately had a salutary effect on the exterior architectural solution: the Morgan House would have a minimally altered fenestration and roof profile. The Thaw Conservation Center was designed by the firm of Samuel Anderson Architect.

6. Serving on the building committee were Trustees Rodney B. Berens, S. Parker Gilbert, chair, Ladislaus von Hoffman, James R. Houghton, Annette de la Renta, Richard L. Menschel, and Eugene V. Thaw. Charles Pierce and Brian Regan were also on the committee.

7. Source: Holl presentation booklet, project archive.

8. Ibid.

9. Ibid.

10. Source: Hardy presentation booklet, project archive.

11. Source: Williams and Tsien presentation booklet, project archive.

12. Ibid.

13. Ibid.

14. The competitors were paid $50,000 for the first round and $25,000 for the second.

15. From a public discussion with Renzo Piano hosted by the Landmarks Preservation Foundation, December 6, 2004.

16. *The Library of Babel.*

17. Presentations were made to the Historic Districts Council (Certificate of Appropriateness Committee), Municipal Arts Society, Landmarks Conservancy (Public Policy Committee and staff), American Institute of Architects, New York Chapter, the Architectural League, Community Board Six, and the Murray Hill Neighborhood Association.

18. In the open position these louvers were reminiscent of Richard Neutra's screens.

19. Several members of the Landmarks Preservation Commission shared this view.

20. Initially there was also going to be paneling in the auditorium foyer.

21. This represented a transfer from the earlier Thaw Gallery, formerly located near the site of the new pavilion.

22. Renzo had already visited exhibitions of drawings, so these other collection presentations built on those experiences and made clearer the scale and nature of the Morgan's holdings.

23. The design firm Potion developed gallery listening stations for music manuscript exhibitions.

24. Many original features of the reading room had been retained over the years. The exhibition room, however, had been renovated extensively. Although its classical detailing appeared to be original to the 1928 building, much of the applied decoration, including the large cornice, dated from 1962.

25. The conversion of a reading room to a gallery meant the loss of an architectural metaphor. When J. P. Morgan, Jr., commissioned the Annex, the first building of the recently created public Morgan Library, his architect, Benjamin Wistar Morris, designed a building with two symmetrical rooms: a reading room for scholars and a gallery for exhibitions, visually enunciating the dual purpose of the Morgan. The institution's identity and purpose would henceforth be compellingly illustrated through the vertical stacking of the new Madison Avenue pavilion: collection storage, public entry, gallery, and reading room.

26. Acoustical engineer Eckhard Kahle of Belgium, in association with David Harvey of Harvey Marshall Berling Associates, based in New York, provided acoustical consulting. In the end, we had to rely on their expertise, track record, and advanced computer modeling and sanguinely anticipate the aural personality of the new hall.

27. Vellum, for Morgan staff, had definite meaning: the dried animal skins upon which many of its most beautiful manuscripts were written and painted. As some were surprised but not unhappy to learn, it is a translucent membrane of clothlike material.

28. A small number of paintings and decorative works was stored at the Frick Collection, while a selection of the Morgan's medieval treasures was displayed at The Metropolitan Museum of Art. Some nonrare holdings, including portions of the reference collection, were housed in a storage center.

29. The vault is constructed to provide for the highest degree of safety for collection storage, including protection from seismic, fire, and flood conditions. Its bedrock location protects it from above-grade cataclysms, and its design was borrowed from submarine technology (a sealed volume within a sealed volume). The vault piers are tied to the bedrock with steel anchors, making it unlikely that the large enclosed volume could become dislodged or buoyant in the event of disastrous flooding.

30. Portions of the north side of the Annex where building fabric had been removed were also restored with new Tennessee pink marble, though, as with the Annex's original construction, the anathyrosis method was not employed.

31. *Stucco* as used here refers to a composite cementitious material that can be scored to look like masonry blocks.

32. It was thought that both the scope of work on the house could be reduced and that it would be a project that was a candidate for support from foundation or other funding sources with a historic preservation mandate. It was always known that the east and south side of the house would have to receive a new face, as much of the brownstone there had been removed when the Lutheran annex and the Morgan's Garden Court were built.

33. The process was known by the straightforward term *match and patch*.

34. As the Morgan prepared to reopen, we recognized that there was a once-in-a-generation opportunity to consider by what name it is known to the public. The museum identity was born with the institution in 1924, when the Indenture of Trust allowed for the possibility of activities beyond those of a research library. J. P. Morgan, Jr., clearly had broader forms of public access and education in mind. At the same time, he was explicit that the legal name was to be "The Pierpont Morgan Library." Over the years, it has been known familiarly as "The Morgan Library," "the Library," and, simply, "the Morgan." Thus, the museum function had not heretofore been captured in the name. Specialists advising us about communications, marketing, and institutional visibility, urged that we better establish the museum part of our identity in the public mind, signifying clearly that there were museum programs and services here. At the same time, we wished to honor the founder's intentions as well as time-honored practice. After much consideration and consultation with Trustees, we concluded that "The Pierpont Morgan Library" should appear at the entrance to the facility and be employed in formal and legal usage. Yet we also determined that it was strategic to add *Museum* for outreach purposes. Therefore, wherever in the recent past we formerly used "The Morgan Library," it would be replaced with "The Morgan Library & Museum" and, wherever sensible, "the Morgan."

35. Imrey Culbert assisted in determining the design of exhibition cases.

36. Landscape designer H. M. White, who was working on the New York Times building with the Piano firm, was retained for the Morgan project.

A Conversation with Renzo Piano

CYNTHIA DAVIDSON

The meeting is running long and late. We are in a Morgan gallery that has been transformed into a workroom displaying a full-scale mock-up of future wall paneling samples and auditorium seating (Fig. 49). Renzo Piano and members of his architectural team are going over several design details with Charles Pierce, Brian Regan, and other Morgan staff. The Morgan team thinks that the proposed red upholstery for the auditorium chairs is not quite right with the cherry paneling. "We can't do this," Pierce says. "Why not?" asks Piano. "Because I don't like it," Pierce replies, a comment received with much laughter. They look at other fabric colors. "I thought red was a happy color," Piano intones. The chair color goes undecided, but Pierce and Piano agree on the color of the stain for the cherrywood paneling and they both sign a sample panel. When the meeting adjourns, Piano, dressed in khakis, a blue button-down shirt, and navy blazer, sits down for a more casual conversation.

CYNTHIA DAVIDSON *I want to start with a little of the history. The Morgan project began with a competition, which you declined to participate in. Why did you decline to participate in the competition but then later accept the commission?* [Piano chuckles.] *I know you do competitions.*
RENZO PIANO No, not really, no. We really don't do competitions, but what happens is that sometimes, for some reason, you are obliged to make a competition, so that is something else. Yes, we have done competitions a long time ago. Beaubourg [Centre Pompidou] was an open competition.

But wasn't the New York Times tower a competition?
Yes, but it was not a competition, and anyway I didn't want to do that competition. I gently tried to explain, but then they insisted. I am telling this story not to say that I'm not arrogant but because making a competition makes me worried. You know, to make a competition you have to put in a lot of energy and a lot of love. It's a bit like falling in love with a lady and then she gets married to somebody else and goes away. It's that kind of thing. It's not worrying about time or money or whatever. I'm worried about that little tiny thing that is essential, and that is passion. You start to do something and you get passionate about it, and then suddenly for some reason that escapes you completely—the bride runs away with somebody else. At my age that's not good. But, yes, the New York Times tower was a competition. It was an invited competition and they asked four architects—me, Norman Foster, Frank Gehry, and Cesar Pelli. I didn't think we should do that competition, then they insisted we should do just a concept and come to a meeting, something like that. And sometimes, a design, a concept, is not actually made, and they ask you just to present your reaction. There are all different levels of engagement. The worst is when you really make a competition and you make real drawings, spend six months.

Did you think that the Morgan competition required more energy?
It was a serious competition.

Even though the scale of the project would seem much smaller?

Oh no. The scale of the project doesn't matter. Sometimes people ask you just to make a sketch, and this is not necessarily much better because a sketch, if you don't want to be a sort of academic formalist, implies some depth. Yes, architecture is art, but it is also social, it is also environmental, it's so complicated that before making the sketch you have to analyze many things, so you get involved anyway. So I said really clearly, it's not because I don't do competitions, not at all. First, we are really doing a lot. I never stop. I'm lucky that I have been busy for thirty years—a miracle. But if somebody says, "I have a job for you," my first reaction, honestly, is "my God, no, no, please no." Because I am so concerned at the moment about two or three things on other jobs and it feels almost like betraying our duty to take another one.

So when the competition was over and the Morgan contacted you, what were your terms for accepting the job?

That was different. When the Morgan wrote to me the second time, Charlie Pierce said he was coming to Italy and wanted to meet with me. He is a very cultivated person, was going to Sicily, I think, taking some holiday and he wanted to meet me. We did not meet then but he explained in a very frank way, because he is a very frank person, that he was canceling the competition for the Morgan project. I didn't accept immediately because normally I never take a job without being at the place, without having understood the context. So, as it turned out, we met first in the Paris Workshop. Then I came to New York on my way to somewhere else, and I came here. I immediately found the idea of holding those three pieces that are historical, demolishing the rest, and creating space for making a little town with many glimpses inside and outside. I felt that very strongly. I didn't know at that time if that was possible, because it was a bit mad. I was simply suggesting to take down everything except the three historical buildings—the Morgan House, the Annex, and the McKim building. Then I did what you should never do if you want to keep your distance: I started to sketch. And once you start to sketch, it's done.

You're engaged.

Yes. Then we started. Day by day, this becomes part of your daily duty, so you don't feel like betraying it with other things. It's a bit primitive, but it's quite true.

When you came to New York and saw the site, had you an idea about the program or was this just your gut reaction?

You're not a countryman. You don't go to a site without knowing something. Yes, our profession is based on inspiration, whatever you like. But it is also based on a great professional approach. You have to understand [the program]. I focused on it during the flight from Paris to New York, which was enough time to absorb and understand the basics. I remember that day on the airplane I also read again a famous little novel of Borges, *The Infinite Library*.[1] Before leaving, I called my friend Umberto Eco, because a long time ago he was telling me about this funny place in the middle of Manhattan where he found a beautiful place that he was passionate about—the Morgan. You know he wrote *The Name of the Rose*. He's a great friend, and we've been working together a long time on many, many things together with Luciano Berio, the musician. So I called him because I remembered that one day we spent an evening in a nice little restaurant in Genoa talking about this idea of exploring, going underground to look for things. And he told me about this. So I called him to say that I was talking with the Morgan about a project. "Oh, that's great, fantastic," he said. "Don't spoil that place. It's a great thing." Then we started to talk about this idea of the safe, of the treasure. And he said, "You remember that piece from Borges? Read it again." Then I read it again. It's beautiful.

I know this story.

The infinite library is a great concept. It's a library made of infinite—not infinite, because infinite is a concept that is *humano,* so it is *almost* infinite—elements. Each room is a hexagon, and they touch each other and they go this way and that way, that way, that way, and that way. So you are where you were before in some way, in that mold where you see and feel down and up. I immediately loved that idea when I came here. Manhattan is made of schist, and if you are lucky enough not to have a river under your foot, if you cut like a knife into it you have the best place to hold and conserve a secret or a treasure against time, weather, vandals, and all that. So all of this came together. I read on the airplane the program made by Charlie and his staff, and I read Borges's ten-page novel again. It's a great, mad idea. Even in my library at home, which is a little one, there is the feeling of safety and security or richness that books give you. I have 3,000 books there, no more than that, yet so much is there. I don't read every day, but it's there.

Is there stone under the Morgan site?

Of course. We have been digging down 50 feet or more in the stone. If you were here six months ago, you would have walked down in the middle of the rock. It made a lot of sense to put the vault in the granite for a number of reasons: practical, psychological, cultural. It was good from the point of view of practicality as well, because we didn't want to build too tall. So this building is a bit like an iceberg with quite a lot below grade (Fig. 50).

Much more below than above?

About equal. An iceberg is about nine times bigger below than what you can see outside; here that's not the case, but we have a lot. And of course what you decide immediately to put underground is a vault, the auditorium, the mechanical room, storage. Immediately it was also clear that it was not a bad idea to have the feeling or sensation that you were walking on a treasure. We actually tried to think about making the vault visible. But in the end, from the point of view of conservation, which is one of the most

Fig. 50. Inside the vault

important duties of the museum—I should say that museums were invented as places to preserve art against everybody and time—this was not really a good idea because we have to keep the books and manuscripts and art in the perfect, dark environment, protected from humidity and temperature and all of that. But also light. If you want to see, that means that you have to allow light to come in. It also became more and more clear that it—a transparent vault—was not secret enough; it was a bit too explicit. Mythologies are sometimes made up of things you don't see, but you know they are there. So I talked again with my friend Umberto Eco. I don't know how to say it. A project like this is not only about designing. It is also about the imaginary. And so we came step by step to the conclusion that it was much better to know that under your feet you've got the treasure. Then, when you go down to the little plaza underneath, you see the vault, but you don't see inside.

But you are aware of the vault?

You are aware of the vault. So this is the big idea. We went through all those steps, including the idea, which was a bit immature, that we should be able to see inside, but it was not the right idea here.

When you came to the site and saw the potential of the village idea, how did you make decisions about what to edit out?

The first thing was clear: we have three historical buildings and we have space for three other new buildings in between. I have always thought that it's quite rare in Manhattan to find buildings that touch the ground in a good way. Manhattan buildings often touch the ground in an arrogant way [*gestures downward*]: THWONGK. Very hard. In this case, the idea was to make a little plaza inside, to have a kind of perception, not mysterious, of exhibition, art, and library. This idea immediately created the other idea. By having three buildings, if you put three new buildings in between them, you complete the village, the little town, but you don't fill the entire space because otherwise you create a barrier. On Madison, between the Morgan House and the Annex, there's only so much space. We wanted to put a building there, so we left a little gap between one building and the other. On 37th Street you have a building that is mostly for offices, and we have a certain space, so we left eight feet on one side, ten feet on the other side. The buildings never touch. This is very simple. To define the width of those spaces, I've been trying to remember the proportions of the little streets, the little *calle* in Venice. My whole country is full of them—well not just my country, even Paris is full of them. As a European you may have a kind of habit to do this. By the way, one way to create tension between something and something else is by inserting something small—a small negative—between them, like a rest in music (Fig. 51).

Will they be passable? Will people be able to walk through them?

Well, it depends. We have one, two, three, four, five, six—some of them, yes, some not. In some we put fire stairs, but they are almost completely transparent, so they are really light. So basically you have the existing buildings, you have the new buildings, and they don't touch, and then you have the spaces. So that means, when you walk on the street, you have the feeling that this building is an institution that is more penetrable, more welcoming, more open, more transparent. But it's not soluble. We also wanted to express the sense of robustness and solidity and protection by making those new volumes in steel. Have you seen the piece of steel we used? It's solid steel, it's not a fake thing, it's solid. So when you look at the little cube on 36th that is going to be a little gallery, 20 x 20 x 20 feet inside, that block of steel is like a little safe. It's a solid piece of metal. So the sense of solidity is there, the sense of protection is there (Fig. 52).

And permeability.

Permeability is almost the opposite, but they are not incompatible.

No. It creates a nice tension.

Exactly. In fact, if you walk on Madison and look through those little windows [in the construction fence], you start to guess how you enter, because you have the volume, and below it you enter and go straight to the piazza.

At one point you had a different grid system for the steel panels. Are you happy with this one?
In the design process we always pass on different options, which is necessary in order to really understand the project. You are not happy or unhappy with these options, because at the end the choice goes to what we think to be correct for this particular circumstance. Actually, the actual grid system chosen corresponds to the first one we designed.

Was it in the program that you should change the primary entrance? How did you come to change the primary entrance to Madison Avenue?
First I should say that this is simply pragmatic. It doesn't matter if the entrance of an institution is very small or intimate, but today you need a lot of function space. Not just information but security, audiovisual, audio guide, the cloakroom, all of those things. So it's not essential to be grand there, it's not about grandeur, it's about space; you need usable space (Fig. 53). The other thing is, I love the idea that you are able to see the entire depth of the institution from Madison through the first block to the little piazza and the garden behind. I love the idea that in the morning the sun is coming that way, the light is shining through like a shade of theater (Fig. 54).

But is it pragmatic when people are used to thinking about entering on 36th Street? The Morgan has to completely reorient the visitor.
It is pragmatic when you have an entrance that provides all those functions. I mean, this entrance has been changed several times. Once you give the strong semantic function of entry on Madison, the confusion will last only a few weeks, and then everybody will be clear that this is the entrance, so I'm not worried about that.

Didn't you have to persuade Charles Pierce that this was the right move?
Of course, of course. But that was a very civilized discussion. In fact, in the beginning everybody was thinking about it and everybody agreed that a sense of permeability—of being readily able to go inside the institution—was essential.

Fig. 53. The completed entrance lobby

Fig. 54. The Gilbert Court interior, facing east

MARCH 2005

Renzo Piano, tall and lanky, walks into a Morgan House basement meeting room—rudely furnished with a makeshift table and an assortment of folding chairs—and pulls off a dark wool coat. It's bitterly cold, but he's been walking the site with Charles Pierce, Brian Regan, and several photographers. The navy blazer Piano wore in autumn has been replaced with a wool plaid jacket, green and tan, worn over a sweater—layers. Despite the cold, he's visibly pleased with the progress on the building.

When we last spoke we were talking about the new Madison Avenue entrance and its space for coats and so forth. But we didn't talk about the fact of it being new in a historical setting; that is, that it means entering something new rather than entering a historic building. The public will enter a new pavilion instead of a historic building. This puts the new before the old. Did you consider that?
Yes and no. The entrance is by definition a space that is open and lined with new functions, so we can't put the new entrance in an old building, that's for sure. The McKim building was out of the question. The Annex entrance was very small, out of scale, and the Morgan House was also subdivided and it's a very old building. So practically speaking, programmatically speaking, it was impossible to find a space for a new entrance in one of the three buildings. The entrance had to be in the gap between those buildings. Actually, we moved the entrance many times, trying to explore different possibilities, and in the end the idea of putting it on Madison was the best one because this was a more clear entry point. The other thing is, when you enter the new pavilion, now you can see on your right the Annex and on the left the Morgan House. They have more of a presence on Madison Avenue than before because there had been a wall there. The new entrance doors will not be in line with the front of the building but set into it (Fig. 55). When you go in the entrance, to the left and right you will see those two old buildings. It will be like, in my best dream, when you realize that cities are made by layers, and the layers come together and don't destroy each other. A new layer, a new building, or a new thing from the nineteenth century is layered on something from the eighteenth century that is layered on something from the sixteenth century, and in the best case they come together and they live together. I think that people will feel that the institution is historical because it doesn't matter where you are—36th, 37th, Madison—you will be able always to see the new inside the old. You remember the plan [*Piano takes a piece of paper and draws the basic site plan again*]. Every time you see a building, a new piece, you see the other one as well. You will see inside. You will see much more than before. The perception, the understanding that this is a mix of old and new, I think will be strong. Yours is a good question, though, because it could have been done in such a way that you don't feel it.

The Morgan has been closed, and when it reopens it will want to seem new. Do you think there will be any shock of the new? (Fig. 56)
The new is three small buildings and a lot of glass filling the gap between the pavilions. When you are in the new building and you look around, you will be able to see through

the entire place. Actually, right now Charlie and Brian and I are freezing because we've been outside talking about the Morgan house finish, the material, the stucco or whatever, which people will see from inside and outside of the Morgan. I don't think people will be shocked. I think people will feel very strongly the presence of the old buildings. Actually, they will be even more present. In the previous situation, for example, you were not able to see the back of the McKim. Now you will. In the new we will feel and see more of the old.

What does the term context *mean to you, and how do you feel the contemporary interacts with the historical? And what does context mean to you, particularly at this site?*
On this site and in this institution context means we have a treasure of rare art and manuscripts and books. We put the treasure in the most safe place you can find in Manhattan, in the rock.

Right, we talked about that before. Do you think that the rock is part of the context?
I think so. And the idea that the treasures are there, in a safe position in the rock. You don't need to see them to feel that they are there. The infinite library is there; you don't have to see each detail in any way. So in some way, history for this institution is not just expressed by its buildings but also by the idea of what the institution is about: to conserve its treasures for eternity, forever. This idea that a museum has a strong and very dignified duty to preserve art forever is a very important element of history. It's actually the soul of the institution. So if you ask me what context is, I think context is also that (Fig. 57).

What does context mean to you above the ground?
Above ground, one of the little dramas was the reading room. I loved the old reading room in the Annex. At the same time, that space was very cramped and we also wanted to increase the exhibition space. We had to think about the new location and the new spirit of the reading room. We decided to put the new reading room on the top of the building on Madison in such a way that it has natural light. In some way, natural light was the way to give magic to the reading room. The old reading room was magic because of time, age. Time makes things beautiful because they become part of our habit. The magic of the new will be natural light, in the sense that the reading room is levitating on the top of the building and getting light from above (Fig. 58). This is also contextual, because this is a very special library. It is not a public library but a place where the art is in the book, so it is extremely important to be able to come here and study. So context seems to me to be the institution itself, not just the vault and the building. Historical buildings are part of the context, but it is more than that. It's the spirit of the institution and this idea of the rare materials and the McKim being a piece of art in itself. In the institution that I saw when I started work on this job four years ago, some of the ideas that are part of the new project were already there. For example, the court,

Fig. 57. Interior of the Clare Eddy Thaw Gallery

the open area that we have in our scheme, a garden court was already there. Now we call it the piazza, but it's the same concept. It was a little more trapped inside the opaque buildings and could feel like a dead end, but the space and light were here. It's a place for conviviality, for community life, for people to come together and to have lunch (Fig. 59). I call this the profane part of the museum because the sacred is the place where you look at art or read books or do solitary activity. But this was already here, so that is another way that the project has a legacy from the conditions I found. Not just the historical buildings, but also the way the institution is stratified in time, including the natural lit space in the middle, which came from the previous building project. We are making it in a different way, we are rebalancing it, but the basic emotion of finding in the middle of the place a space with natural light was a very good idea. This is just to tell the truth, because that garden court space was there. It was not necessarily working well, but it wasn't bad and the new piazza is a kind of homage to that garden space.

Fig. 58. The Sherman Fairchild Reading Room

(*Following pages*) **Fig. 59. The Gilbert Court, looking north**

If you get your sense of magic from a place or some of the things we've talked about, the history of a place, does any of this affect an aesthetic approach for you? Do you feel more comfortable working in a particular palette today than another? Or are you flexible in terms of materials or an aesthetic?

My conviction is that every scheme is so different that you must be really silly to believe that you can apply the same logic and the same signature every time. This is essential. I am completely convinced that the concept of style is a big trap. When you start a new job, if you are worried about imposing your style, your rubber stamp, it's a very bad beginning. When you start a new job you have to establish the palette, as you called it, you have to understand the spirit.

I like the idea that when you start a job you establish it in a totally free way, even free from yourself, from your habits, from your formula, if you have any. I mean, I don't think architects should have a formula.

You don't have to have a formula, but you might be more comfortable working one way than another. Then what you have is a language. You have your own way to write. I may have my own language to build, but it's not a formula. Formula is when you write an essay the same way. It's flat. Or like a filmmaker who does a love movie and a war movie the same way—

it's ridiculous. But this happens to everybody, because this is the trap of success. Once you are successful in doing something, then people want you to make the same thing again and again and again, and you get trapped. So in some way the freedom you have to defend most is not really freedom from others, it's freedom from yourself. The risk is that you may fall into the trap of becoming self-referential. This is why morally, ethically, culturally speaking, I love the idea that when I start a new job I am free. I walk around, and I try to catch the spirit of the job, the spirit of the people, the spirit of the place, the little genius loci, all those things.

Do you think that when someone who has some familiarity with your past work comes to the Morgan that he or she will say, this must be another Renzo Piano building?
Maybe, but I don't care. I remember somebody going somewhere once and saying, "I'm sure this was one of your buildings." But this is not because we repeat the same formula. It's because we have the same eagerness for transparency sometimes. If you go to the Menil Collection, or other buildings, they are so different. At the same time, you can feel something that is a constant. But it's not the way I struggle to make a building. I don't care about being recognizable. When I first came here, it was quite evident from the beginning that this place was first, about beautiful, important treasures; second, it was historically important because the three historic buildings were part of the legacy; and third, I found this idea of having a space trapped in the middle like a little piazza. Just to talk about another job here in New York, the Whitney Museum, not very far away. I knew the Whitney before, but when I started working on it, I went there and spent hours, days, walking up and down, trying to catch the spirit, trying to understand what else we could do, trying to invent a new way to get in the new institution, a bit less difficult than the present. So every time, every project is a new story.

The Whitney is very different from the Morgan, both the site and the program.
Everything is different. But it's even more different when you move somewhere else. When you move up to Harlem and start to work on the Columbia western extension, or when you are in Times Square and Eighth Avenue and the area of Broadway and you have to design the headquarters of a newspaper like *The New York Times,* they are all completely different. Every time you try to build up your palette. And the palette is never just about material and color, it's also about human beings and social invention and working conditions and whatever. That's why architecture is so interesting, because it is a very complex discipline where everything comes together. It's art in some way, but it's also science, technology, anthropology, social life. All those things come together.

Is there any particular spirit that we would find is common to these structures? For example, will the spirit at the Morgan be substantially different from the Whitney?
Well, the Whitney and the Morgan are museums, so they have something in common. For example, they have the same need of calm and serenity and silence, and at the same

time to be a joyful place to meet people and to stay together. Urbanity is probably the little red line linking those four jobs in New York. Urbanity. It means that all four jobs, socially speaking, are made in order to create a place for people to live, to meet, to be, and to enjoy life. To build a sense of urbanity means to build a sense of conviviality, the joy of being together and sharing the same passion. Socially speaking, I think this is something that you will find in the New York Times, in Columbia, in the Morgan.

You find this all the way back to the Pompidou, no? This is a theme in your work.
Yes. In some way, this kind of social anxiety—this desire, this *langue de social*—is a desire to change the world. In some way, architects need to have this kind of mad, unreasonable utopian idea that you can change the world. So yes, maybe this is there. It was in Pompidou, it was in many other schemes.

Well, some would say you changed the world with the Pompidou.
No, no. But anyway this is the unreasonable idea that you have to have, otherwise, why should you be an architect? Forget it. Anyway, this is talking about social life. But if you ask me about what kind of common denominator you can find, maybe it is a certain desire to explore new materials and new technology and new structure. I was born the son of a builder, and this left a strong impression in my hands. I loved the idea that an architect is also a practical person. He's a practical person that actually puts his hands in the matter and tries to put together pieces. Somebody may think that this is just stupid technology, but it's not. You know, every artistic gesture, creative gesture, comes down to practical things at some moment. Even playing the violin is about vibration and the strength you put into it. *Techne,* if you use the Greek word, which is more noble than *technology,* is part of creation. And then, on a completely different plane, is the one of expression. Probably the common denominator of those jobs is fighting gravity. I mean, this idea of lightness—I like lightness, I like the idea of transparency. Well, I also love massiveness, because sometimes you need that, but in some way I can see the advantage in and the beauty of lightness. Lightness first, because it's a kind of constant challenge (Fig. 60).

I want to go back to Borges's idea of the infinite library. You talked about how the infinite library is infinite spatially, but of course there is no infinite space in this library. I want to turn to the idea of time and the old space/time equation in architecture. Is it possible to have infinite time in a place like this? In a library?
As you understand, I was joking. Because in fact nothing is infinite, not even the library. Because this story is so good that it didn't talk about a real infinite but magic.

You were joking, but you were also serious.
Yes. What is great about the infinite library, apart from the dramatic composition of the hexagons and the stairs and all that, is the idea that everything is there, everything

(*Following pages*) **Fig. 60. The Gilbert Court ceiling**

already written and to be written in the history of humanity. Now of course nothing is infinite, but every time I think about the vault of this institution, I have the feeling of something that goes deep into history. This is why I felt that that story was beautiful, because of the sense of abundance of words, all those books coming from so far away. But it's more than words. For instance, have you seen the Morgan's music manuscripts? You can also see the history of humanity in them. When you look at a Mozart manuscript, you realize that this guy was incredible. He was writing music like I write a letter to my daughter. Everything is there in that sense.

How does your addition to the Morgan contribute to the sense of time or perhaps timelessness that one feels here?

The building is done in such a way that it will last forever in some way. When you make such an institution, it's mad, but you have to think about that. You have to think about something that in the year 3000 will still be there. I found recently new information about this big meteorite, called 1950 DA, that will fall on earth in the year 2880, in 875 years, so it's far away, but it will fall unless between now and then we find a system to divert it. It's funny, because when I found this information, it touched me a lot, I am making a joke, but I am also serious—especially since I have done some something like the Morgan, a building that should last a thousand years or more. I know it's a bit mad, but when you make something like the Morgan, it must be done in such a way that it will last forever. Because eternity is exactly the function of a museum, which takes a piece of art away from running time and puts it in a new dimension that is timeless. This is the spirit of a museum. A museum is to conserve art forever, for eternity. So eternity, that is, the infinite, is not an impossible dimension of architecture. This is what you have to think about. When we were cutting into Manhattan schist deep down in the earth, the idea related to this was eternity. To dig down and put the rare materials in such a place that they may be there forever. So yes, yes, I know it is completely insane, I know it's completely unreasonable, but that's the way you have to approach it.

What is the hardest challenge you faced in designing the Morgan scheme?

To build something that has to respect the history of this institution and that is in harmony with the spirit of this specific site. At the Morgan they always mention the "ethos" of this historic institution. Well, we think that this project respects all this. We have not designed a huge building, everything respects the scale and the history of this particular site, and yet, we are improving all the functions and the functionality of the institution. In this case, the risk was to be monumental, too big, out of scale. We really think this did not happen.

1. Jorge Luis Borges. Also translated as *The Library of Babel.*

Becoming The Morgan Library & Museum: A Historical Interpretation

PAUL SPENCER BYARD

THE VILLA MORGAN

A villa is a building in the country designed for its owner's enjoyment and relaxation . . . the pleasure factor is what essentially distinguishes the villa residence. . . . The villa is typically the product of an architect's imagination and asserts its modernity. . . .

—JAMES S. ACKERMAN, *The Villa*[1]

It's not a "reading library," said Junius Morgan emphatically to Charles McKim in May 1902, expanding on Morgan's instructions for his new library. It's a collection of rare volumes, "rarities or curiosities," he said, behind glass but in low bookcases "easily reached," with space for "bric-a-brac" on top.[2] The tone was set. The treasures were not for scholars, at least not right away. They were to generate immediate pleasure, to be touched and handled or contemplated and caressed with the eye. In the quiet, isolation, and near gloom of his new library, smoking his cigar in his Renaissance chair—often with the logs in the huge Renaissance fireplace smoking beside him—Pierpont Morgan would enjoy himself, take his ease in the company of the friends of his leisure, the exquisite rare books and works of art he had collected (Fig. 61).

Morgan was very much a man of his times, a big man with large appetites and a strong sense of the righteousness of his conduct and exercise of his power (Fig. 62). He and his contemporaries were serious about their righteousness. Over the course of Morgan's lifetime, the authors of the Sherman Act and the Progressives had begun to argue that there might be a public interest separate from the one he and his contemporaries thought they embodied, but even toward the end of their time, Congress showed its respect, at least toward Morgan himself. These men were serious about their pleasure as well. Much as they might enjoy it, the men of his times who rode their horses into dinner weren't doing so lightly. It was an exercise of their power to take their pleasure as they chose. Morgan was surely among the "finest" of them, with the sharpest eye, the highest taste, and the greatest power, likely to take his pleasure as he particularly chose, at the highest level, in his treasures. Like many of his peers, he saw his self-fulfillment in historic terms. In the exercise of his power, he was turning the United States away from its parochial manifest destiny toward the west and picking up from Europe—not as a usurpation but as the most natural thing in the world—the lines of power that ran the world as a whole. With Morgan's help, the United States was succeeding to world history and Morgan was succeeding European popes and princes— the historic powers—to the highest of the world's pleasures. His library would, among other things, mark in its own way the new world leadership of the United States.

Charles Follen McKim was the embodiment of the transformation of American architecture at the time. In 1893 he had led the great turn of the World's Columbian Exposition away from the eclectic confusion of the Gilded Age to secure the place of U.S. architecture into the classical succession reflected by the European Beaux-Arts (Fig. 63). No matter that it was world's fair architecture or that its classicism was trow-eled on. No one suggested that it was any less authentic or correct for the United States.

Fig. 61. The West Room, Pierpont Morgan's study

Fig. 62. Pierpont Morgan at Dover House, 1902

In connection with the exposition, Frederick Jackson Turner had decreed the closing of the old American frontier. The architects of the dazzling-white exposition proposed an impressive new representation of the United States as a world power. It was no coincidence that the next great manifestation of the change was the global cruise of Admiral Dewey's impressive new white fleet.

McKim and his firm were essential to the expression of the change. In 1895 his partner, Stanford White, simultaneously bulked up and tamed Jefferson's delicate prototype University of Virginia—just right for the infant republic of 1820—into a new model powerhouse appropriate for higher education in the United States at the end of the century. McKim then derived from it a new prototype for Columbia University as the United States set out to become a force in the world (Fig. 64). In Boston, McKim tied the United States to Europe in his palazzo for the public library. At Symphony Hall, he reproduced the old Music Hall—a fascinatingly close if eccentric adaptation of Europe's great Leipzig Gewandhaus—but cleaned up and squared off as if to make it formally presentable by the new standards of the day.

When Morgan called him about the library, McKim was heavily involved in a project that went the other way, embedding the United States in Europe. Unlike the other nations that had academies in Rome—France, for example, which took over the Palazzo Farnese—the United States would build its own American Academy in Rome as if to go

Fig. 63. Agriculture Building, the World's
Columbian Exposition, Chicago, 1893

Fig. 64. Low Library at Columbia University

Fig. 65. The American Academy in Rome

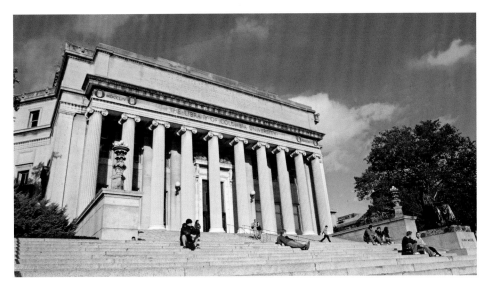

out of its way to show that it belonged, to show Europe how to do better something Europe had done for years (Fig. 65). Furthermore, unlike the other academies sponsored by old nations, the American Academy would be sponsored by men like Morgan who were making the United States into the new world leader.

When he called McKim, Morgan had already tried and failed to find a proper architectural expression for his library. Whitney Warren, architect of the marvelous baroque stern of the New York Yacht Club on 47th Street, had missed the mark with an ornate pavilion that confused the riches of profusion with the high worth that pleased Morgan (see Fig. 13). McKim's first try also missed the mark. It looked more like a small, elegant bank or suburban branch library, like McKim's own Free Library for Orange, New Jersey (Fig. 66). To the extent that with its little institutional portico it looked like a library, that was exactly not the point.

Then McKim hit the note that made the library the success it is. He prepared Mr. Morgan for it, telling him it was the product of "months of study" in the two letters in his hand that set up its unveiling, describing the design in terms flattering to Morgan.[3] The letters show McKim, the experienced architect, setting up his meeting to get what he needs to hear, establishing and then rescheduling it when he hasn't got his act together, when he doesn't have the cost estimate he could hardly expect to see Morgan without. They also fit with McKim as a genuinely anxious man, particularly stressed by the project and Morgan.

What McKim unveiled was a slightly raised freestanding horizontal block of marble with no windows in front—a treasure box—with a nearly flat facade held together in the middle by the key to its meaning, the serliana at the front door (Fig. 67). McKim would probably not have called it a serliana. He got it from Rome, from the nympheum of the Villa Giulia and from the facade of the Villa Medici. At the Villa Giulia the serliana is a

decorated opening on the second story (Fig. 68), suitable for a loggia like the one Stanford White put on the Century Association on 43rd Street (Fig. 69). In the Villa Medici, the serliana is the entry (Fig. 70), not unlike the one McKim gave the Walker Art Museum at Bowdoin College (Fig. 71). In each case the device made a connection with a villa—again the proper reference for Morgan's library—and, best of all, with Rome. There it connected Morgan with Pope Julius III, a world power like Morgan and, as the patron of Michelangelo, pretty close to the top of possible art patrons. The device also made the connection with the Medici, the greatest name in banking and finance, at least until Morgan.

As James S. Ackerman points out, the device was invented by Donato Bramante and popularized by Sebastiano Serlio and is best known now for its association with Andrea Palladio. Palladio used it most memorably as the entry for some of his most radical villas (Fig. 72).

These are the breathtakingly strange lumps of masonry with which Palladio helped recapture Venice's terra firma by making a productive country life attractive and rewarding to wealthy Venetians. The villas were also the principal vehicles through which Palladio revealed his astonishing expressive invention, what architects a generation after McKim would see as the modern concept of form.

What's interesting about the device is that it's almost incapable of being institutional. Part of the reason is that it is naturally recessive, a shadow in the middle that calls attention less to itself than to the mass around it, an invitation rather than a proclamation. The serliana can be a way into a *tempietto*, it can be a way into Bowdoin's Walker Art Museum—itself a monumentalized Vincenzo Scamozzi villa—but it won't ever carry the curse of the portico that one can imagine doomed McKim's first scheme. More important, perhaps, is simply that the association with Palladio attached it to his villas as seats of personal, not institutional, pleasure and power. Set up and back from

36th Street in a suggestion of a freestanding palladian form, the serliana was just what McKim needed to establish the library, not as an institution apart from Pierpont Morgan, but as an extension of his persona. Once again, like so many big men of his age, Morgan would be doing good by doing right by himself.

While the connection with Palladio enabled McKim to keep the building Morgan's, the architect fairly clearly wasn't interested in Palladio's humanism—the sporting out-door equality of men and gods the frescos of Tiepolo and Veronese offered as the reward for helping Venice. He wanted something more instructive and heroic. What mattered to McKim, as he wrote to Morgan in his letters before the unveiling, was that the library would be a monument to Morgan. He wasn't just saying it: monumentality

Fig. 70. The Villa Medici, Rome

Fig. 71. Walker Art Museum, Bowdoin College, Brunswick, Maine, 1894

Fig. 72. Villa Poiana by Palladio, Poiana, Italy

would not just be a side effect of its size or an incident of its beauty. For all its intimacy as a private library, the structure would celebrate Morgan as, if not larger than life, at least as large as life could get. Thus McKim's serliana grew as big as he could make it, set in a frame that breaks out ever so slightly above the cornice line of the block. A flat panel like that of the Villa Medici, his serliana then is importantly set off by ever so slight reveals from what are articulated on either side of it as the symmetrical ends of imagined flanking wings, as if seeking to gain authority for the facade by suggesting it is backed up by a larger, symmetrical building. From its slight elevation the false front of the Villa aims its lessons straight at the world. In the middle, the serliana comes as near as it can to a triumphal arch.

Fig. 73. The Manhattan Appellate Courthouse

It is in this monumentality, this celebration of his patron, placing him in the long pageant of historic power down from Rome to the United States that McKim showed his modernity, the special insight of his times as he saw it, that we were the heirs of Rome. The form of the building—so important to Palladio and then to the moderns—didn't matter much. The rooms inside were going to be unequal and wouldn't fit in the block. No matter: they could stick unevenly out the back (see Fig. 14). What mattered was the beautiful, correct, formal, historic announcement on the front that made this personal library into something right for a world historical figure in the United States at the turn of the twentieth century.

Two novelties added to the sense of continuity with Rome. The first was the whiteness of the marble of the Villa, not quite the dazzling imperial white of the World's Columbian Exposition—or even of the exposition's first white offspring, New York's exquisite Appellate Division Courthouse, finished a few years before on 25th Street and Madison Square (Fig. 73)—but still an ancient white, an antique monument white that set the building off from its relentlessly brown neighbors as something both ancient and new, a little like the historic ruins revealed emerging from the earths of time in a Piranesian view of Rome. The second was something you could hardly see but caused an equal or greater amazement. This was McKim's feat of retrotechnology, his experiment with anathyrosis. It's fascinatingly consistent with his reverse modernity that McKim should have gone back more than two thousand years to the Erechtheum for his only technical innovation. Thus he proposed to Morgan that the building be a demonstration of antique dry masonry construction not seen for two millennia, with marble so perfectly cut it would need little or no mortar. After inquiring as to the extra cost, Morgan went along, possibly humoring McKim and possibly also endorsing this added degree of correctness. Thus they adopted for his monument the ultimate antique right way to go and made clear that as successors of the ancients, Americans were tech-

nically just as good or better. McKim ordered squeezes, or models, of the original joints to show how smooth the effect would be, and the wax impressions sent back from Europe delighted everyone. When it came to contracting, the ambitious, if innocent, contractor accepted the challenge for the same reasons—this was the way to please Morgan and McKim and show how terrific he was, even if it set him up for a significant financial bath. McKim's gesture may have been a little precious, but it added to the sense of the Villa Morgan and its contents as treasures beyond price.

The design process was not, of course, entirely about the facade, but also about the rooms inside: the large book room, Morgan's smaller study, the small but luxurious librarian's office, and the central rotunda that held them all together. One of McKim's singular achievements was that he got the relative proportions of these different rooms of such different sizes and heights to work so well together. A great deal of thought went into the stylized muralism of their decoration, with Henry Siddons Mowbray contracted to provide it. The bookcases were important as were lighting and ventilation. Much correspondence attended the choice of various decorative borrowings from Europe—including the somewhat mysterious European ceiling for Morgan's study that McKim had quietly arranged to have completed and improved by an American hand. Then there was the sculptor Edward Clark Potter's extended struggle to find the right posture for the two slender catlike lionesses—forebears of his famous lions for the New York Public Library—commissioned for the upslope of the stair to the front door (Fig. 74).

The exchanges between Morgan and McKim were not entirely smooth. Morgan growled a lot, enough to frighten McKim and lead Augustus Saint-Gaudens to urge McKim for his own good to talk back. Morgan was categorical: Mr. Morgan "does not wish to have . . . absolutely will not accept" were typical directions. Morgan was blunt: "Your letter was not what I wanted."[4] No wonder McKim broke down for a while during the project. No wonder he wrote to Stanford White with such obvious relief when things went well that "the skies are blue. . . ."[5]

McKim's breakdown was a significant interruption and Morgan's refusal to accept Stanford White as McKim's surrogate a revealing detail. Morgan simply may have been loyal to McKim, but he may also in his own complex Episcopal moralism have had reservations about White. The process yielded a design that went to bid to contractors and was completed without major incident beyond bad weather and delays from strikes. Morgan in fact took possession before the library was finished. There is no formal statement of what it meant to him.

To understand that, we have to imagine what it was like for him to use it. First of all, we have to remember the formality of his relationship to it. While there was a tunnel between his house and the library, it was almost surely for service, not for Morgan himself. To use the library, he had to put on his hat and coat, go out the front door of his house onto the sidewalk, turn left, and walk. It wasn't exactly a trip to the country, but it was a definite disengagement from ordinary domestic life. When he got to the gate, he turned again, addressed the entry, and started up the truly delicious steps with a ratio of tread to riser that virtually floated him up past Potter's alert felines. The steps took him into the maw of the serliana and to the knobless antique doors that would have been opened like magic by an alerted servant using an enormous key. Imagining Morgan a solitary figure under the arch at the top of the steps in homburg or top hat, addressing the tall double doors alone or followed by an entourage, you feel the high art of McKim's architecture—the choice of the serliana and the management of its expression—that makes the structure at once Morgan's personal villa and monument. It supports the monumental reading to recognize that the virtually windowless treasure house with its tall bronze doors and its references to antiquity is also somewhat tomblike.

When the doors were opened for Morgan, he stepped into a private world of, for him, perfect sensual reward, with everything rich and correct. When he entered, he might have found the Villa already inhabited by the nymph that went with it, that fascinating mixture of sensuality and correctness he made its librarian, Belle da Costa Greene. All around were the richest of materials completely in order. Mowbray's ceilings personified virtues as upright men and women correctly revealed in Roman clothing (Fig. 75), not one with a lock out of place.

The Villa seems to have had two flaws. The first was that the fireplaces sometimes didn't seem to draw. A furious Morgan thought it was a design defect. McKim thought Morgan's servants or Morgan himself simply didn't know how to lay a fire. Then there was the lighting, the single attribute that must have made it clearest that Morgan's wasn't a "reading library." Somewhere in the process of fitting out the book room, it lost its principal east window to make room for yet another treasure, a tapestry. Even allowing for differences in technology and for our own rising expectations for interior light, with its few windows and electric lamps the Villa must have been truly gloomy

Fig. 75. Rotunda mural by H. Siddons Mowbray

(Figs. 76 and 77). The gilding of the bindings and frames, however, must have been particularly alluring when they caught such light as there was. The low light didn't serve the reader, but it did serve the sensualist.

It was, above all, Morgan's villa and it worked for him. He used it alone for his pleasure—again, it's easy to imagine him in his study thinking in the dark with a cigar by the fire. He does not seem to have entertained in it apart from its purpose, inviting friends and official visitors in to see his treasures, sometimes accompanied by him, sometimes, like William Howard Taft, not. For privileged, invited bibliophiles, it was a bookman's paradise, as *The London Times* correspondent said at the time over many glowing column inches. Then Morgan also used it for business, so much so that it came to be known as his uptown office. As an office it must have had a very particular effect. It wasn't as if you had been invited to Morgan's house, with distracting reminders of other people's lives. A visit to the intensely concentrated library would have had attributes of a visit to an important prince, to a royal treasury thrown open for a visiting head of state, to please him, of course, but also as part of a deliberate strategy to take him in, impress him, and bring him into line. The men of Morgan's time felt it right to show their wealth. Mr. Morgan showed his less than many of them, but he did so with a purpose.

Fig. 76. The East Room under construction with windows in the east wall

Fig. 77. The East Room with the windows covered

The library had a certain atavism as a seat of power, the sanctum of someone who, looking to get what he wanted, could flash his gaze, as Edward Steichen put it, like an oncoming freight. The half-dark of the treasury, the privilege of penetration, must have set you up to go along with what he asked. When Morgan famously forced a solution to the Panic of 1907, the Villa surely did its part.

THE ANNEX

If the original library made sense as the Villa Morgan, in the end it didn't make sense without Morgan himself, and it must have seemed more than a little anomalous after he died in 1913.

It took a while to sort out Morgan's affairs, to come to terms with the fact that the monument he had put together could not be kept together without him. Thus when major works of art from the library went on the block and were pounced on by Frick and others, it was possible to feel that Morgan himself was diminished. The library's functional weakness as a scholarly resource wasn't addressed for some years. The project to rectify the weakness came early in a very different world, after the imperial catastrophe of the First World War brought about the end of white fleets and grand alliances and the sense of righteousness—the mixture of entitlement and virtue—that convinced the big men of Morgan's era that serving themselves was serving the public interest. Specters hovered abroad as a result of major changes—the bloodshed of the war, the Bolshevik revolution, the latent power of a collapsed, resentful Germany. There were now other constituencies to be served. The idea of Morgan and what he stood for in fact became a target and symbol of breakdown and change: in 1920 an anarchist's bomb aimed at J.P. Morgan & Co. made a bloody mess of forty bystanders, wounded hundreds of others, and chipped 23 Wall Street. "Remember we will not tolerate any longer," said the American Anarchists Fighters.[6]

Architecture had moved with the era. Beaux-Arts was no longer the wave of the future. Now it stood for the status quo ante, what so many conservatives worked hard to bring back after the war, and it had lost most of its heroism, possibly because of the kind of horrors its manly heroism had brought to the world during the war. People were beginning to recognize the need for change and choices for architecture, particularly in Europe, where inklings of modernism suggested radical new directions for progressive movements and the architecture that would serve them. Even imperial architecture had taken on a very different cast in works such as Edwin Lutyens's moving Thiepval memorial or his powerful viceroy's palace (Fig. 78). The choices hadn't much penetrated New York, but the atmosphere was transforming into one that didn't so unquestioningly venerate connections with the past.

In 1924 J. P. Morgan, Jr., called Jack, accelerated the evolution of the library, by giving it to the "public," along with an endowment, entrusting the management of its assets to a board of trustees. When a friend of the family wrote to praise him for the magnanimous gesture, he quickly wrote back to say that he did it more as a memorial

to his father than as a benefit to his "fellow man." He then began the process of designing the new building, or Annex, that would work better for his fellow man. As a site for
it, he chose to take down his father's house on the corner of 36th Street: the personal
Morgan would yield further to the institutional. He chose his own architect, Benjamin
Wistar Morris, of Morris and O'Connor, who had designed Jack's house in Glen Cove
and whom Jack felt had done a particularly good job memorializing his grandfather in
the Morgan Memorial annex to the Wadsworth Atheneum in Hartford (Fig. 79). It also
cannot have hurt Morris to have been a relatively little boy at St. Paul's School when Jack
was a mighty upperclassman. On behalf of McKim Mead & White, Lawrence Grant
White expressed "regret" at the choice.[7]

Morris himself had trained at the Beaux-Arts but was also, within the limits of his
gifts, becoming open to choice, unlike McKim Mead & White, who at their peak offered
a choice of suitable traditional styles brilliantly and correctly done. Choice here included
possibilities of novelty. Morris was later at least associated with the genesis of one of
the century's greatest innovations and successes: his is the design for the Metropolitan
Opera House in Hugh Ferris's famous first rendering of Rockefeller Center. He also did

Fig. 80. The Cunard Building, New York, 1921

the Cunard Building on lower Broadway (Fig. 80), the Brearley School on the East River, and, at the end, the pleasantly dowdy interiors of the first *Queen Mary*.

Morris's first design for Jack Morgan was close to a clone of the Villa (Fig. 81), a block like it with a flat cornice set at a height just below the Villa's and a flat facade relieved by pilasters and a tall front door set close to the plane of the facade. The block would have been set back from 36th Street—a step toward the country again—with a forecourt and paths dividing around a fountain leading to a double stair. The building would have shared the irregularity of the original—a large reading room to the right, a smaller gallery to the left, a rotunda in the middle—but might have rationalized it with a significant square cloister behind. The cloister might have been ornamented with ever-so-slightly progressive 1920s statuary.

Morris was addressing, possibly with the idea of the cloister, the chief technical problem of the design: how to attach to the original Villa. The old building was meant to be freestanding and freestanding it was, to the point of orneriness. Morris solved the problem with a corridor from the notch in the back of his new design to the notch in the back of the old building, probably over the old service tunnel. The corridor in this position was kept low and set well back from the street, far enough to help maintain the apparent autonomy so crucial to the identity of the older building (Fig. 82). This connecting corridor meant that the public visitor would always sneak into Morgan's original library from the back corner a little like a servant—a difference of status built more or less forever into the experience of the Morgan by the resistance of the old Villa.

Fig. 81. An early design proposal by Morris for the Annex

Fig. 82. The cloister, depicted in 1960, before the addition of a second story

Fig. 83. The Boston Public Library, 1895

Meanwhile Jack was not altogether pleased with Morris's first proposal. If it in fact seems weak, it is possibly just because it so nearly replicates the Villa that it doesn't get the point that the Annex is supposed to be something different. Morris revised the design, simplifying the entry, moving it closer to the street and, at Jack's suggestion, giving it a roof like the Boston Public Library (Fig. 83). Conscious or not, Jack's invocation of McKim's great public library was an appropriate bridge for the change of character and function he had set in motion for his father's library toward public use. Morgan and Morris agreed to use Tennessee pink marble but not to extend McKim's experiment with anathyrosis, settling for plain ashlar. They discussed at length mottoes to go over the entry door, Morris suggesting one that pointed out virtues of having money. Morgan vetoed it: the time for praising wealth publicly had passed. Now the door would simply identify the new institution.

To be sure the new building went properly with his father's, Jack specially ordered a rendering of the buildings seen together (Fig. 84). In the first rendering, the Annex was seen from the point of view of the Villa. In the next, the point of view shifts to the west; the more ordinary, institutional Annex takes the lead in the foreground, and the richer, stronger, more beautiful but now frankly less relevant Villa moves to the back. The final design of the Annex seems handsome but a little indeterminate, as if it can't quite figure out what to make of its corner site. Its classicism is more than a little mild, perfectly correct but lacking the old prewar conviction. Morris himself called it "a modest harmonious foil." [8] But as such, it represented the library as it now saw itself quite accurately. The front door and vestibule were still quite elegant and narrow. You were still on your best behavior; nothing was yet thrown open to the public. Inside the visitor

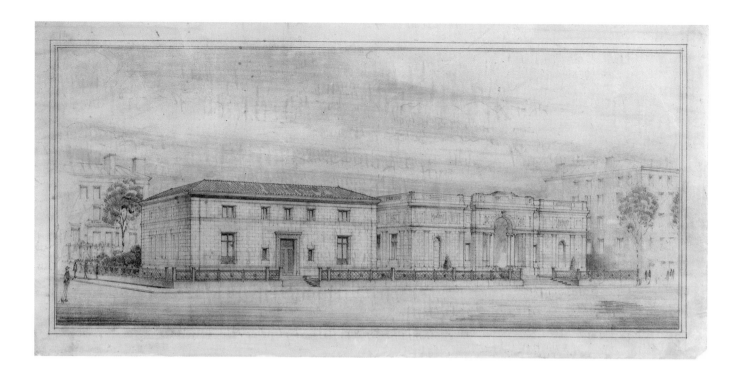

got ceiling paintings by the aging Mowbray (Fig. 85) and a facility still highly formal
and possibly familiar in its layout—and still animated by the same custodial spirit,
Belle da Costa Greene—but much better adapted to use not just for pleasure but as a
scholarly resource.

THE PIERPONT MORGAN LIBRARY

It's not clear how quickly with the addition of the Annex the institution became The
Pierpont Morgan Library, or "the Library." There is evidence of orders at the very end
of its construction that as a general policy no visitors were to be shown through the
"Main Building."[9] With visitors forbidden to use the front door of the Villa, the Annex
would in fact have taken over from the "Main Building" and established the experience
that would characterize the Library for the next sixty years. The Library thus started

Fig. 86. The Exhibition Room, before 1950

Fig. 87. The Exhibition Room after alterations in 1962

the modern era after the war with the institutional and architectural balance Jack had suggested between public (Annex) and private (Villa), and it evolved slowly thereafter in the direction he had set—and his father had anticipated—from the private toward the public. The Depression was not a time for action, even for an endowed institution. Pressures for change came largely from the increasing services the Library slowly undertook to provide as a scholarly resource, putting more material on display, offering more reference services, adding staff. Pressure also came from the outside, as public power intensified during the Depression and the public began to assert its interest where it contributed to the private benefit. Thus the grumblings in the early 1940s of Mayor Fiorello H. LaGuardia bringing pressure on the Library to justify its tax exemption, sending a young representative of the Corporation Counsel[10] to read the guest book and be sure the Library served a public beyond such luminaries as the queen of Rumania, who indeed had visited the Library.

Architectural changes were limited to efforts to find space in the building for expanding functions related to scholarship, with some modest concessions to increased public use. During the late 1940s, an effort to put more material on exhibit was rejected by the Trustees partly out of fear of atomic attack, a reminder of the early Cold War, when atomic attack was something for which one thought one could rationally prepare, in this case by keeping things not on display but under cover. The initiative was revived in the 1950s and yielded the 1960s changes to the Annex designed by Alexander P. Morgan, a member of the family, with Morris's successor firm, O'Connor & Kilham. The goal was simply to squeeze more into the Annex, lowering the ceiling of the entry lobby and the gallery (Figs. 86 and 87), to make more space on the floor above, including a rather stiffly formal lecture room (Fig. 88). This generated what was the major perceptible change, the doubling of the height of the connector between the Annex and the Villa and its ornament with a fairly confident single classical window in the middle (Fig. 89). The Annex and the Villa were now that much more firmly stuck together.

At the very end of the modern era came the only significant change to the appearance of the Annex (Fig. 90), an addition of some thirty feet in the back by William and Geoffrey Platt. Coming when it did, in 1974, the thoughtful classical extension drew critical comment as an early example of postmodernism. William Platt was outraged: "it's not postmodern; it's premodern!"[11] The architecture of the Library, that is, had made it through the modern era virtually untouched.

What did touch it, though, were all the complex forces that took over in the postmodern period with the general abandonment of the modern social project in the late 1960s and early 1970s. The emergence of museums as broadly popular destinations was a development of great significance to the Library. Whereas it continued to grow in stature as a scholarly resource, that growth was now paralleled in the world at large by a new interest in museums not as scholarly resources or objects of collective pride but as venues for numerous individual epiphanies in connection with works of art. As the collective modern public interest faded and was replaced with the self-interest of

Fig. 88. The Meeting Room was created as part of the 1962 additions.

Fig. 89. The exterior of the cloister, now doubled in height, depicted by Schell Lewis, 1960

Fig. 90. Annex addition, after 1962

postmodern individualism, museums evolved to meet the new demand from individuals who now came in crowds.

In this context, the Library took its next steps to meet its own internal needs. When the Lutheran Church put Jack's house on 37th Street up for sale, the Library bought it and converted it to use for offices and conservation facilities. The house (see Fig. 91) was a handsome period piece, a rich evocation of Pierpont's era—a turn back for the Library toward what the Annex had tried to move away from. After years of uncertainty—following a famous legal proceeding, the Lutherans had considered tearing the house down—everyone was delighted it would be saved. The Library restored the house, a highly popular move in a period increasingly preoccupied with historic preservation, and added facilities to meet and take advantage of the new demand for popular contact with its treasures. A glass-enclosed Garden Court (see Fig. 7) connecting the house to the Annex was built. The Garden Court by Voorsanger Architects was everything a good postmodern work of architecture was supposed to be: light, white, friendly, with a wave-form glass roof that didn't take itself too seriously and created a very pleasant quasi-outdoor greenhouse. The project resolved thorny issues of accommodation for the handicapped that had become legal requirements with the new emphasis on popular access.

By buying the Jack Morgan house and building the Garden Court, the Library did vastly expand its capacity to accommodate visitors, at least those who came for the experience of the Library and its exhibitions. And it helped meet its need for support space for offices and conservation. Primarily a Library, however, the Morgan wasn't exactly in the position of a museum to do its work through exhibitions. It still had to conserve its treasures in vaults and on shelves and then give scholars and amateurs a chance to sit

down and study them. And it was in a position of significant architectural confusion. It now had two front doors, the visitor-friendly one off Madison Avenue leading through the Morgan House to the Garden Court and the more serious, now somewhat old fashioned and stuffy one off 36th Street through the Annex to the reading room (Fig. 91). Three separate buildings of considerable self-importance now spoke for the Library in very different voices, mostly about private life in the past, and the connecting architectural material lacked the strength and presence to make sense of what they said, let alone suggest the Library's institutional direction. The evolution anticipated by Pierpont Morgan and launched by Jack was at a turning point. Was the Library just a charming surviving semiprivate oasis, or was it indeed an important cultural power? Was it time to come out as one of the great institutions that make life in New York significant?

In 1999, in moving to commission architecture, the Library took the road chosen during the last decades of the twentieth century by virtually every significant arts institution seeking to provide for growth and institutional clarification: it held an architectural competition. In the Library's case, the competition was private and never publicized. Like institutions in its class for seriousness and public purpose, it chose a distinguished advisor, Paul Goldberger. With him it made a short but strong list of representatives of the high postmodern architectural imagination—a chance to consider the identity that imagination could give the Library. The senior anchor of the list was Hugh Hardy with forty years of cheerful, somewhat theatrical institutional additions, many involving historic buildings. From the next generation, Tod Williams and Billie Tsien had shown the elegant possibilities of an adventurous high seriousness at their remarkable Neurosciences Institute in La Jolla, California. Steven Holl was the nearest to an emerging master, capable of the startling beauty of the St. Ignatius Chapel in Seattle and the seminal strangeness of the Kiasma Museum in Helsinki, an architecture that opens the way to a different perception of the world. The Library wanted one name for the list to fill out its range, but the great homo faber, or "man the maker," Renzo Piano, made a point of generally choosing not to enter competitions.

The Library gave the competitors an expansive view of its needs, making it clear that they should treat its existing inventory of old buildings with the utmost respect. Beyond their inherent value, two of them were designated landmarks of the City of New York and, in the intensifying conservatism of the very end of the century, any whiff of irreverence might bring down torrents of abuse. To add necessary space to the composition of old buildings, the Library authorized the competitors to recapture the space of the Garden Court, to demolish the Platt addition to the Annex, and to put the entry to the new assembly on 36th Street. The choice seemed obvious. It kept the Library connected to the relative intimacy of 36th Street, made the new building plainly a backup for the Annex and Villa, and seemed most respectful to the Villa, giving the arriving visitor the handsome frontal lesson put forth by McKim.

The competitors gave the Library what it had on the face of it asked for. Williams and Tsien were the boldest, adding to the assembly of old buildings a new block of space lifted into a new dimension, marvelously cantilevered over everything (see Fig. 21). Steven Holl twisted the needed spaces into the assembly in a fascinating evolution of the Kiasma form (see Fig. 19). Hugh Hardy chopped into it a sound and solid, somewhat corporate interior amplification (see Fig. 20). The Library found itself uncomfortable with all of the results and gave the competitors the opportunity to rework their schemes in response to its comments. Williams and Tsien went the farthest converting their cantilever into a slender glass tower (see Fig. 25). Steven Holl was the most reluctant to change what already seemed like a winner. Hugh Hardy offered two new schemes, one corporate or something simulated old and brown.

The Library then had a most unpleasant bullet to bite. Not really liking what it got—however clearly it had asked for it—it could go forward with what it had set in motion, largely because it had set it in motion, or it could stop. It could become what this architecture would make it, whether that was what it wanted to be or not, or it could try again. To the intense distress of the competitors, in a serious demonstration of institutional bravery, it stopped. And then it wrote to Renzo Piano.

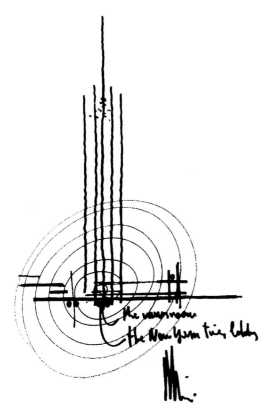

Fig. 92. Renzo Piano's design sketch for the Times building

Fig. 93. The Kansai Airport

THE MORGAN LIBRARY & MUSEUM

The turn to the Renzo Piano Building Workshop was, among other things, an important turn away from late-twentieth-century postmodernism toward a different kind of architecture. Piano was working in New York on the New York Times building (Fig. 92), a project he won in, ironically, a sort of competition. Significantly, the other architects, including the wonderful Frank Gehry, the chief of the high postmodernists, were farther out and more critically favored. A force in Europe since the Beaubourg, Piano had first shown New York in 1992 at the invitation of the Architectural League. He had brought intelligence, invention, and grace to daunting contemporary problems like the Kansai Airport (Fig. 93) and was exceptionally good working with old buildings. He was very much a maker of things: his office was a workshop that made models of buildings as tools of human service. And it seemed to matter that he was Italian, a man who brought with him the enduring modernity of Renaissance humanism.

What Piano also brought the Library was a lot of intelligence and a certain bravery. Instead of going up for more space—exposing the Library to the preservationists' horror of height—Piano went down into the Manhattan schist, adding that it would protect the objects. Possibly most important, he moved the main entry to Madison Avenue, turning the Library away from its private past and attaching it like a major institution to a main artery of the city. He did it, he said, to make possible the piazza he organized in the middle of the new assembly of elements (Fig. 94). He also surely did it to end the institutional uncertainty started with the Annex about what the Library was and where it belonged. In moving the entrance, far from disrespecting the Villa, he seemed to understand and take it at its word, to put it back as McKim and Morgan intended it, out of the world, not in it.

Fig. 94. The Gilbert Court

Then, in composing his addition, he showed himself the master he is of this kind of design. To cohere the Library's three dissimilar boxy parts, pulling different ways and saying different things about the institution, he added not one but three more parts so that the old ones had to say what they said as voices in a larger democracy of six. Set in the same scale, the new parts, which also were boxy, imparted an abstract elegant modernity, and together all parts spoke about where the institution was going, not where it had been. With extreme tact, the old parts were outvoted.

Piano used the new parts to adjust the relative weight of the assembly. The largest and clearest was in the middle, over the entry, addressing Madison, a beautifully proportioned abstract announcement of the new direction for the now renamed Morgan Library & Museum, with its pinkish white panels just as windowless and impenetrable as the Villa, quietly but firmly in control. Then he used the parts as an inventory of objects that could be placed between the old objects like asterisks to set them off, to help them be clearly themselves while participating in the new more numerous group. The opaque new entry box had reveals of glass on either side to distinguish and connect the Morgan House and the Annex. On 37th Street, Piano made a little office tower, again with a reveal to set off and define the back edge of the house. Then on 36th Street, he made up a box for which there was no programmatic need except the crucial one—to solve at last the problem of connecting the Annex and the Villa. Now his elegant little cube gallery replaced the limestone blur of Morris's and Alexander Morgan's hyphen connector and, with glass reveals on either side to let in light, reestablished the Villa and Annex as independent contributors to the larger group. Holding them all together was the extraordinary volume of the public "piazza" that finally transformed the Morgan into a very special kind of public space. Piano's scheme was a paradigm of the best design with good old architecture: the photograph of his fingers inserting the assembly into the model of the old buildings became the poster for the Historic Preservation Program at the Columbia University School of Architecture Planning and Preservation.

Here at last, then, was The Pierpont Morgan Library now become The Morgan Library & Museum, a new New York institution with all its old parts working together but in a new common direction. For all its new presence and public access, its architecture kept it private, a "library" of old and new building volumes, with much of the interiority of a book that you have to read to get into. And what a world inside! The passage under the resistant panels to the explosion of rare, pure, serene interior volume became one of the major cultural experiences of the city.

The magic of the design from the point of view of historic preservation had to do with its understanding and handling of the meaning of the Villa. The Villa looked better than ever—even with tiny added shadows where the lead sheet in the joints had squeezed out over the years—clearly set off now from the Annex with nothing much over or around to suggest the change except the new shots of sight into the central piazza. And the new entry was precisely not through it or next to it: the Villa was left alone on its side street, the way it was meant to be, with the public brought around

Fig. 95. The Seattle Public Library

to enter from the roaring avenue. The Villa was still entered through the servants' entrance, with due respect for the old hierarchy. We weren't given the entry experience Pierpont Morgan reserved for himself or used to impress his visitors, but we came to them from the new interior volume that was beautifully ours, as treasures that now belonged to us. The transformation came from the inside out, with the books and art and old buildings arranged around our space for us to seek out and take in. The elegance of it—the rare emptiness of the central volume, the small, exquisitely lit galleries and reading room it led to, the revelation of the collection treasure by treasure—were all Pierpont Morgan. The Morgan Library & Museum was ours.

The architecture became the Morgan as an institution devoted to human culture and, as importantly, it helped the Morgan move into a position of leadership. Stood up against the high postmodernism of Rem Koolhas's Seattle Public Library, for example—the beefy grid, the you-asked-for-it, you-got-it novelty (Fig. 95)—the Morgan reminded us of different human qualities. The Morgan now stood not for Pierpont Morgan's wealth and taste but for the contents of his books—the best contents of the human mind—and for the redeeming human enterprise of reading and trying to live up to them. There was nothing merely monumental or "gee whiz" about it, only the brainy kind of "wow" that came with the recognition of its metaphor. Graced with an architecture of exceptional intelligence, in times that manifestly need a new direction, the Morgan now invited us to expose ourselves to the treasures of the mind and think, and showed us all around what thinking might do for us.

1. James S. Ackerman. *The Villa: Form and Ideology of Country Houses,* Princeton University Press, 1990, p. 9.

2. Junius S. Morgan quoted in Herbert L. Satterlee, Esq., letter of May 19, 1902, Department of Prints, Photographs and Architecture Collections, New-York Historical Society (N-YHS).

3. McKim to Morgan, February 28 (no year, 1904?), Morgan Library Archives, Box 1381 – Wills File.

4. Letter of Pierpont Morgan, November 19, 1904, N-YHS.

5. Typed note of McKim to Stanford White, February 1, 1906 (?), N-YHS.

6. Quoted in William Bryk, "Big Bang on Wall Street," NYPress, March 1, 2001, p. 2.

7. Letter of Lawrence Grant White to Charles Moore, Esq., February 16, 1928, N-YHS.

8. Letter from Benjamin Wistar Morris to McKim Mead & White, May 28, 1926, N-YHS.

9. Note, July 1928, N-YHS.

10. The representative was Spencer Byard, Esq. (the author's father).

11. Conversation with Charles A. Platt, March 2005.

1. James S. Ackerman. *The Villa: Form and Ideology of Country Houses,* Princeton University Press, 1990, p. 9.

2. Junius S. Morgan quoted in Herbert L. Satterlee, Esq., letter of May 19, 1902, Department of Prints, Photographs and Architecture Collections, New-York Historical Society (N-YHS).

Credits

Every effort has been made to trace copyright owners and photographers. The Morgan apologizes for any unintentional omissions and would be pleased in such cases to add an acknowledgement in future editions.

PHOTOGRAPHIC COPYRIGHT

Page 114, fig. 68, Allinari / Art Resource, NY; p. 111, fig. 65, American Academy in Rome, Photographic Archive; p. 111, fig. 63, Avery Architectural and Fine Arts Library, Columbia University; p. 125, courtesy of the Boston Public Library; p. 115, fig. 71, courtesy of Bowdoin College Archives, Brunswick, Maine; p. 111, fig. 64, Columbia University; p. 112, Library of Congress; p. 14, fig. 5, Museum of the City of New York, Underhill Collection; p. 123, Collection of the New-York Historical Society, negative #80231d; p. 13, p. 14, fig. 4, p. 15, p. 20, p. 22, fig. 11, p. 24, fig. 13, p. 24, fig. 14, p. 27, fig. 16, pp. 38–41, p. 42, figs. 23–25, pp. 56, 72–73, p. 119, p. 124, fig. 82, and pp. 127 and 129, The Pierpont Morgan Library, New York; p. 126, fig. 84, The Pierpont Morgan Library, New York, 1958.25; p. 122, fig. 79, The Pierpont Morgan Library, New York, ARC 302.1; p. 23, The Pierpont Morgan Library, New York, ARC 1456; p. 110, fig. 62, The Pierpont Morgan Library, New York, ARC 1496; p. 120, fig. 76, The Pierpont Morgan Library, New York, ARC 1578; p. 108, The Pierpont Morgan Library, New York, ARC 1590; p. 25, The Pierpont Morgan Library, New York, ARC 1591; p. 110, fig. 61, The Pierpont Morgan Library, New York, ARC 1616; p. 120, fig. 77, The Pierpont Morgan Library, New York, ARC 1758; p. 117, The Pierpont Morgan Library, New York, ARC 1797; p. 113, The Pierpont Morgan Library, New York, ARC 1802; p. 130, The Pierpont Morgan Library, New York, ARC 1931; p. 27, fig. 17, The Pierpont Morgan Library, New York, ARC 2024; p. 131, The Pierpont Morgan Library, New York, gift of the Charina Foundation, 2007, ARC 725; p. 126, fig. 85, The Pierpont Morgan Library, New York, gift of Mr. and Mrs. Hugh Jones, 1989.24; p. 124, fig. 81, The Pierpont Morgan Library, New York, gift of Mr. Robert B. O'Connor, 1976.31:1; pp. 45, 48, 52, p. 55, fig. 32, pp. 59, 61, 65, p. 133, fig. 92, p. 133, fig. 93 © RPBW; p. 115, fig. 70, p. 115, fig. 72, Scala / Art Resource, NY; p. 136, photo courtesy of the Seattle Public Library; p. 22, fig. 10, reprinted with permission by Joanna T. Steichen.

PHOTOGRAPHY

Page 131, Bernice Abbott / Commerce Graphics, NYC; p. 111, fig. 64, Eileen Barroso; front cover, Richard Cadan Photography / richardcadan.com; frontispiece, pp. 6–7, 18–19, 46, 53, 66–67, 77, 82–83, 86, 88, 90–91, 92–93, 95–97, 99–100, 102–3, 106–7, 134 © Michel Denancé, 2006; pp. 12, 32 © Michel Denancé, 2007; p. 28, Todd Eberle © 1996 Todd Eberle; back cover, pp. 16–17, 50–51 © 2002 Todd Eberle; pp. 72–73, 74 © 2004 Todd Eberle; pp. 62–63 © 2005 Todd Eberle; p. 133, fig. 93, Kawatetsu; p. 55, fig. 33, p. 60, A. Klemmer, 2002; p. 69, fig. 43, A. Klemmer, 2003; p. 69, fig. 42, p. 80, A. Klemmer, 2004; p. 114, fig. 69, p. 116, Schecter Lee, 2007; p. 15, fig. 7, p. 119, David A. Loggie; p. 122, fig. 78 © Andrew D. Pickles, 2007, www.jimmy-spiers.co.uk; p. 70, Frank Prial, Beyer Blinder Belle Architects; p. 27, fig. 16, Clarence White; pp. 72–73, Joseph Zehavi, 2004; pp. 24, 124, 126, 129, Joseph Zehavi, 2007.

PUBLISHED BY THE MORGAN LIBRARY & MUSEUM

Karen Banks, *Publications Manager*
Patricia Emerson, *Senior Editor*
Rose Miesner, *Editorial Assistant*

Project Staff
Christine Nelson, *Drue Heinz Curator of Literary and Historical Manuscripts*
Marilyn Palmeri, *Photography and Rights Manager*
Marguerite Dabaie, *Project Assistant*
Joseph Zehavi, *Photographer*

Designed and typeset in Dante by Katy Homans
Printed by Thames Printing, Norwich, Connecticut, on Galerie Art Silk Text
Bound by Acme Bookbinding